LIBRARY OF THE EARLY CIVILIZATIONS
EDITED BY PROFESSOR STUART PIGGOTT

Civilizations of the Indus Valley and beyond

THE IN

McGRAW-HILL BOOK

CIVILIZATIONS OF
ΟUS VALLEY
AND BEYOND

Sir Mortimer Wheeler

COMPANY · NEW YORK

DESIGNED AND PRODUCED BY THAMES AND HUDSON

© THAMES AND HUDSON LIMITED LONDON 1966
REPRINTED 1972
ALL RIGHTS RESERVED
THIS BOOK OR PARTS THEREOF MAY NOT BE REPRODUCED IN ANY
FORM WITHOUT WRITTEN PERMISSION OF THE PUBLISHERS
LIBRARY OF CONGRESS CATALOG CARD NUMBER: 66–16977
PRINTED IN GREAT BRITAIN
69506

CONTENTS

PREFATORY NOTE

This essay was published originally in 1961 but it is now issued in a revised and enlarged form. In the interim appreciable new evidences have emerged, more particularly with reference to the Indus Civilization: its distribution, its dating, and the circumstances of its ending. Indian, Pakistani, British, French and American investigators have all been busy upon these matters; and since the problems are those of one of the three pioneer civilizations of the world, it may be hoped that the results are of some general interest.

For new information I am indebted to the Archaeological Survey of India under the Director-Generalship of Shri A. Ghosh, and the Pakistan Department of Archaeology under the Directorship of Dr F. A. Khan. Certain of the universities, which are now increasingly active in the archaeological field, have also assisted, and I would extend my special gratitude to Professor Nurul Hasan of the Muslim University of Aligarh, and Professor H. D. Sankalia of the Deccan College, Poona. I would further add my thanks to M. Jean-Marie Casal, of the Commission des Fouilles Archéologiques (Paris), and to Dr George F. Dales of the Pennsylvania University Museum, both of whom have been working actively in the Indus Valley and beyond.

MORTIMER WHEELER

London 1965

1　The Indo-Pakistan subcontinent

CHAPTER ONE

Introductory

Civilization, in a minimum sense of the term, is the art of living in towns, with all that the condition implies in respect of social skills and discipline. An approach to this condition is represented by open villages not later than the fifth millennium in the foot-hills of northern Iraq and by a substantial town at Çatal Hüyük, near Konya in southern Turkey, not later than 7000 BC. But, at the time of writing, the oldest known town dignified by defences – a stone wall and tower and a rock-cut ditch – is Jericho which, on Carbon-14 datings, was a going concern early in the eighth millennium. Jericho occupied 10–12 acres around a covetable spring in the arid Jordan valley, where settled inhabitants might early find a need for the jealous guarding of their precious water-supply and their closely circumscribed economy. Future research will amplify the picture, but Jericho, carried back, as it now is, even beyond its civic state to an underlying meso-lithic village, is likely to retain a high measure of significance in the story of social evolution.

On a wider landscape, too, the hint offered by Jericho is reasonable enough. In the Old World the principal food-grains (except rice, not known much before 1700 BC) and the principal herd-animals subsist or subsisted in a wild state in Western Asia, between the Himālayas and the Mediterranean. It is a corollary that large-scale food-production was first practised in that region; and the first towns, with their primary dependence upon food-production, are the natural sequel. In other words, food-production and town-life began in Western Asia, and not later than the eighth millennium BC. (In this context the possibility of the independent invention of food-production at some later date or dates in America and indeed elsewhere is not considered.)

I have used the word 'town' for early Jericho, and do so with deliberation. As the evidence stands, the site had a closely packed population within formidable defences, and an evolved administration is implied. In common usage, however, 'civilization' is held to imply certain qualities in excess of the attainment at present ascribable to Jericho. More particularly, it is held to include a systematic method of accounting, so that revenue and wages may be adequately registered, and orderly government ensured. *Writing*, in some form or other, is on this view a presupposition. There is perhaps a tendency on the part of the modern mind to over-estimate the value of literacy; certain it is that the unscribbled brain is capable of remarkable feats of retention and calculation. But let it go – the somewhat arbitrary addition of writing to the qualifications of citizenship makes at least an easy yardstick and may lend precision to our thinking.

On this basis, civilization may still be claimed to have emerged first in Mesopotamia where, in the latter half of the fourth millennium (Uruk Period), temple accounts were first kept in pictorial and other signs inscribed on clay tablets. In space and time it is alike proper that Mesopotamia remain our main reference-point in any review of the birth of civilization south of the Himālayas.

CHAPTER TWO

The Indus Civilization (c. 2500–1700 BC)

The Beginnings

There, beneath the Himālayas, arose the primary phase of evolved city-life, named from the location of its first-known and largest sites the Indus Valley Civilization. Discoveries by Sir John Marshall and his colleagues after 1921 gave to India something approaching an additional two thousand years of rich prehistory, and to the world the largest of its three most ancient civilizations. Current exploration both in India and in Pakistan is still adding materially to our understanding of the Civilization, and I propose in the following pages to integrate the new with the old without excessive particularization. The results will be a somewhat modified and indeed extended view of the subject, covering roughly the third and second millennia BC, with brief notes on the sequel in the first millennium.

As to the immediate ancestry of the Indus Civilization there is indeed comparatively little (in 1965) that is new, although the old evidence has from time to time been flogged into a somewhat unreal semblance of life. The general nature of that evidence is tolerably clear whilst its details remain elusive. Briefly the position is this.

In the fourth and third millennia, the Iranian plateau, riven by sharp uplands and tumbling steeply to the flanking riverine plains of the Tigris-Euphrates and the Indus,

Ill. 2

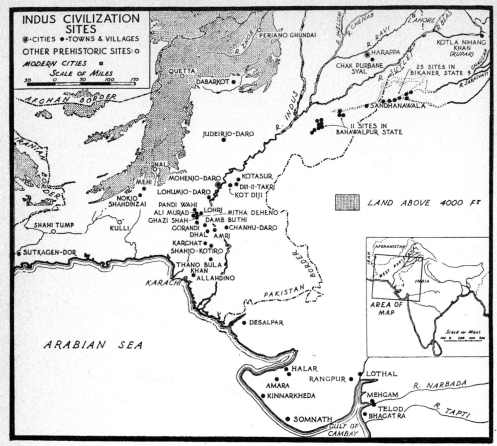

2 'Indus Valley' sites, excluding Kalibangan, 100 miles south-east of Harappā, and Alamgirpur, 600 miles east of Mohenjo-daro

was the home of a multitude of disparate societies, essentially neolithic but verging gradually upon a stone-bronze (or chalcolithic) technology. Fed by animal husbandry and a little agriculture, their villages were sufficiently durable to develop into mounds or *tells*, though some degree of nomadism may be suspected as in similar communities today.

To this widespread village-society it has been customary to trace the primary urban development of Mesopotamia. There the 'Ubaid culture, on the eve of the mature Babylonian civilization, has been traced to likely origins to-

3 Mohenjo-daro originally included an artificial mound or citadel, up to 50 ft high, which stood beside a chess-board plan or lay-out of oblong housing blocks. This view across the excavated streets and houses shows the later Buddhist stupa which now crowns the citadel and dominates the site. The mound beneath the stupa has not yet been excavated, but the theory that the Buddhist shrine may cover an Indus Valley temple is unlikely since nearly 2000 years intervene

wards the east, possibly through Susa, and its westerly extension has been ascribed, with a secure imprecision, to 'some sort of expansive force and internal readjustment' affecting the tribal communities of southern and central Persia. Basic differences between the Indus and Mesopotamian civilizations bar the possibility of any closely related colonization of the former from the latter; and at the same time our knowledge of the Ganges and central Indian cultures is sufficient to preclude an origin farther east or south. We are left with the Baluch or Iranian borderland as the immediate source of the Indus Civilization, at any rate in its more material aspects. Less material but equally significant facets may reflect a somewhat different story.

13

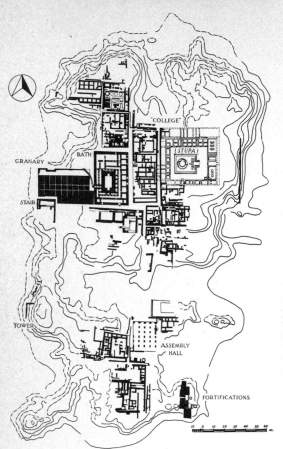

4   Plan of the partially eroded citadel of Mohenjo-daro

Mohenjo-daro and Harappā

First, however, something must be said of the shape and substance of the Indus Civilization itself. It is at present best known from its two largest cities, Mohenjo-daro (or Moenjo-daro) beside the river Indus in Sind, and Harappā, beside a former course of the tributary Ravi, nearly 400 miles to the north-east in the Punjab. Both cities were upwards of three miles in circuit, and both seem to have conformed with certain distinctive and evolved principles of urban planning. Mohenjo-daro was commanded by an artificial mound, perhaps a citadel, up to 50 ft high, which occupied a flanking unit in a chessboard lay-out of oblong blocks (see below, p. 18). At Harappā, a corresponding

Ills. 3, 29

5, 6 Clay missiles, such as the group illustrated opposite, roughly baked and weighing 6 ozs each, may have been projected by slings. Deposits of these and of larger clay missiles weighing 12 ozs each had been assembled as 'ammunition stores' behind the brick parapet between two towers at the south-east corner of the Mohenjo-daro citadel. The standing figure shows where these were found and indicates the size and excellent preservation of the parapet at this point

mound has been identified, and presumably overlooked a similar street-plan in that much-disturbed site. The mound at Mohenjo-daro was fortified by a baked-brick wall and solid towers, of which the earliest in a group excavated at the south-eastern corner had had built-in timbering. On the summit of the mound the known structures included a carefully constructed bath or tank, jacketed with bitumen; and, beside it on the steep verge of the citadel, a high brick podium or substructure which had carried a large timber granary above intersecting ventilation channels. Half-way up one end of the granary was a loading-platform above a recess into which the grain-wagons could be driven from the adjacent countryside.

Ills. 5, 6

Ills. 7–9

Ills. 10, 11

Ills. 12, 13

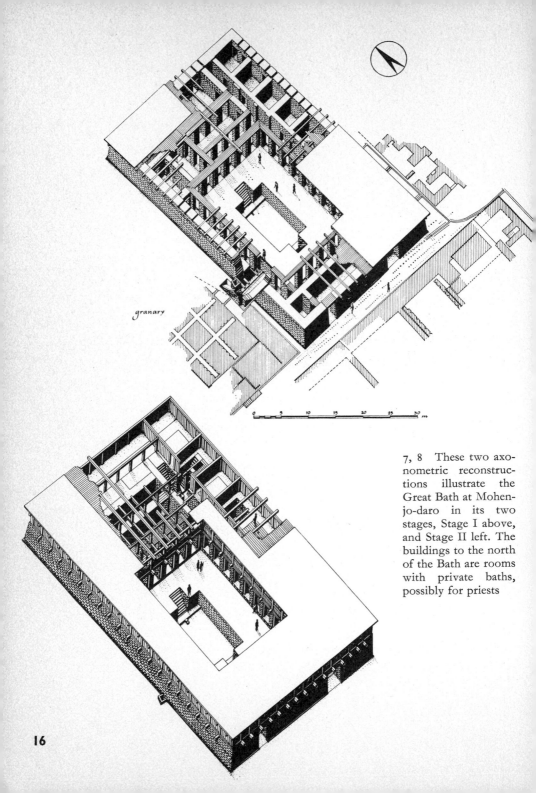

granary

7, 8 These two axonometric reconstructions illustrate the Great Bath at Mohenjo-daro in its two stages, Stage I above, and Stage II left. The buildings to the north of the Bath are rooms with private baths, possibly for priests

9 At the north and south ends of the Great Bath at Mohenjo-daro brick steps with their timber treads set in bitumen or asphalt led down to the floor of the bath, which measured 39 × 23 ft. Asphalt was also used for waterproofing the bath itself. Near the south-west corner an outlet led to a high corbel-vaulted drain, which cut across the loading-bay of the granary, indicating that the bath was of a later date. As shown in the reconstructions opposite, verandahs enclosed the bath and behind three of them were rooms, in one of which was a large double-lined well, presumably the source for the bath

Like the south-eastern tower, the podium had been inadvisedly reinforced by timbers which had decayed anciently and had been partially replaced by brick patches. Nevertheless, the tall solid structure, necessarily accessible and marginal by right of its primary function, must have constituted also a substantial strong-point in the citadel's defences.

Amongst other buildings on the mound were two pillared halls, a series of cells and baths (presumably for ritual purposes) beside the Great Bath, and a long building (230 × 78 ft) which was identified by its excavator as 'the residence of a very high official, possibly the high priest

Ills. 7–9

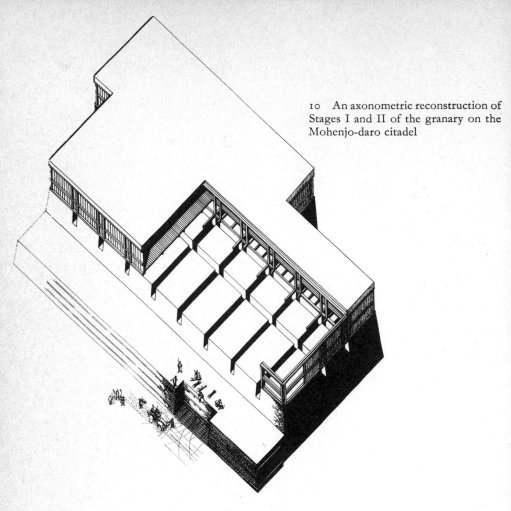

10 An axonometric reconstruction of Stages I and II of the granary on the Mohenjo-daro citadel

himself, or perhaps a college of priests'. One guess is as good as another, but certainly this was no ordinary house. Much work remains to be done by future excavators, but enough has been cleared to show that the citadel was both a religious and a secular headquarters: with the prototype of the ritual tanks of medieval and modern India, halls of assembly, and the State Granary which, in the economics of those times, may be equated with a modern State Bank. The general indication of combined kingly and priestly rule fits the habit of the third millennium.

Ills. 14, 15   Below the citadel the town stretched in orderly array to the Indus, which has moved some two miles eastward

11 The granary at Mohenjodaro was built on a high podium with ventilation passages, and originally consisted of 27 blocks of brickwork with a criss-cross layout of passages. It was later enlarged and partially rebuilt, with a brick stair leading to the upper parts

in more recent times. A branch of the river may anciently have traversed the town itself. But for the most part the urban lay-out showed, from the earliest period yet identified, a remarkable regularity; constituting indeed the oldest example yet known of systematic town-planning. Broad streets from south to north were crossed by others at right-angles, and the blocks thus formed (seven have been identified and others presumed, each some 400 × 200 yds) were subdivided by lanes parallel or at right-angles to the arterial streets. The houses, often substantial and sometimes of appreciable size, consisted typically of rooms round a courtyard and contained stairs to a former

Ills. 16, 17

12 The granary stood on the steep verge of the citadel at Mohenjo-daro and at the western end of its north side was a recessed unloading bay. The figures hauling the sack up with a rope indicate the present size of the structure; the other figure (top left) is crouching in the opening of one of the ventilation ducts. Originally there was a reinforcing interlace of timber and the holes and grooves left after the decay of the 5-inch square beams are clearly visible

Ills. 18, 19 flat roof or upper storey, a bathroom, sometimes a well,
Ills. 20, 21 and occasionally a privy on the ground or upper floor, similar to privies found in Mesopotamia (for example, in the Akkadian palace at Tell Asmar). Throughout, the
Ills. 22, 23 streets and buildings are marked by the brick drains

13 This reconstruction of the granary at Mohenjo-daro is closely based upon the archaeological evidence as can be seen by the remains illustrated opposite. The bullock-carts are of the type still to be seen (*Ill. 62*) and are very similar to the toy carts found at Mohenjo-daro (*Ill. 56*). The means by which the sheaves were hauled up into the granary is conjectural, but there is little doubt that this was the method used .

which are characteristic of the Civilization, both at Mohenjo-daro and elsewhere, and, with their trim inspection-holes, are the most elaborate of their kind in ancient Asia. In its prime, the whole city bespeaks middle-class prosperity with zealous municipal controls.

Ills. 24, 25

21

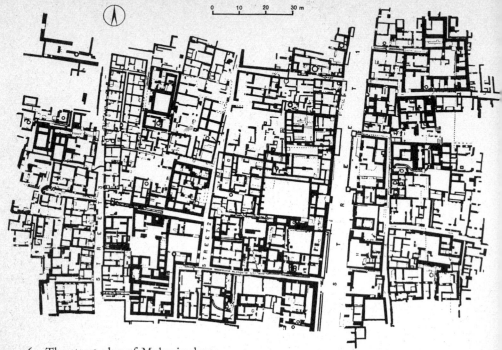

14–16   The street-plan of Mohenjo-daro
above shows part of the residential quarter;
this is the 'HR Area' marked on the over-
all outline plan below left. Below right, a
typical narrow lane in 'DK Area'

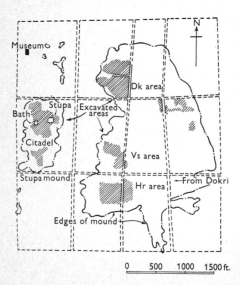

17–19 The basic lay-out of the residential quarter of Mohenjodaro was that of a gridiron. Main streets were about 45 ft wide with narrow lanes, as above, dividing the houses. A feature of the houses was their windowless outer walls; the doors opened on to the narrow lanes rather than on to the main streets. At a late period ovens or kilns were occasionally built inside the town. A typical example is illustrated right. Wells are common at all periods. They are noted for the fine brickwork, as in the example below right

20–23 The high quality of the sanitary arrangements at Mohenjo-daro could well be envied in many parts of the world today. They reflect decent standards of living coupled with an obviously zealous municipal supervision. Houses sometimes had a privy on the ground or upper floor connected with the attendant drains and water-chutes which in their turn gave on to the main sewers. Brick drains are characteristic of the Indus Valley Civilization, both at Mohenjo-daro and elsewhere. They are elaborately designed even to the extent of having trim inspection holes

24, 25 The curious baked clay triangles ('votive cakes') above were probably used for toilet purposes and have been found frequently in drains. They are characteristic of other Indus Valley Civilization sites, *e.g.* Kot Diji and Alamgirpur. *Ill. 25*, right, shows a typical drain, with well-set edges, in a narrow lane with a right-angled turn at its end

Temples have not been clearly identified, but further examination would probably reveal two or three in the areas already excavated: notably, the so-called 'House A1' in the 'HR Area', where a small but substantial oblong structure is approached by an outer gateway and two symmetrically disposed stairs parallel with the frontage, and has yielded fragments of two stone sculptures. Elsewhere in the same Area (in B 5) a regimented block of cells has been regarded variously as a priests' college with an adjacent temple and as a police-station! Once again, much further excavation and more analytical recording are alike necessary. Shops, including one with floor-sockets

Ill. 14

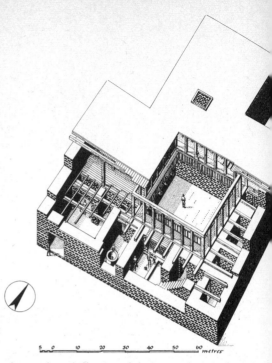

26, 27 A typical covered drain running the length of a street on the citadel at Mohenjo-daro. *Ill. 27*, right, is an axonometric reconstruction of a house in the 'HR Area'. The doorway leads into an entrance-room with a tiny porter's lodge; through this lies the courtyard, with the household rooms opening off it. This house is in the extreme north-east corner of the plan, *Ill. 14*

Ill. 28

for large jars, can be recognized along the main streets; the private wells are supplemented by public wells, accessible from the streets and lanes; and here and there are small 'sentry boxes' for the civic watchmen. Construction is normally of baked brick in 'English bond', unbaked brick being confined almost exclusively to the internal platforms with which the builders strove to keep the floors above rising flood-levels. Most of the brickwork was originally covered with mud-plaster.

Ills. 29, 33

Harappā was plundered more than a century ago by railway-engineers, but the general outline of the citadel has been recovered, with a few fragments of the street-

28 The conical hollows sunk into the floor of this room may have been dyeing vats, but were more probably holders for jars in a shop or public restaurant. The room is part of a large building; it measured $87 \times 64\frac{1}{2}$ ft and living quarters were provided around a courtyard

plan. The fortification of the citadel mound consisted of a mud-brick rampart tapering upwards from a 40-ft base, with a similarly tapering external revetment of baked brick. In the 300 yds which intervened between the mound and the river were barrack-like blocks of workmen's quarters, serried lines of circular brick floors formerly with central wooden mortars for pounding grain, and two rows of ventilated granaries, twelve in all, marshalled on a podium. The total floorspace of the granaries was something over 9000 square feet, approximating closely to that of the Mohenjo-daro granary before enlargement. The whole lay-out, in the shadow of the

Ills. 30, 31

Ill. 32

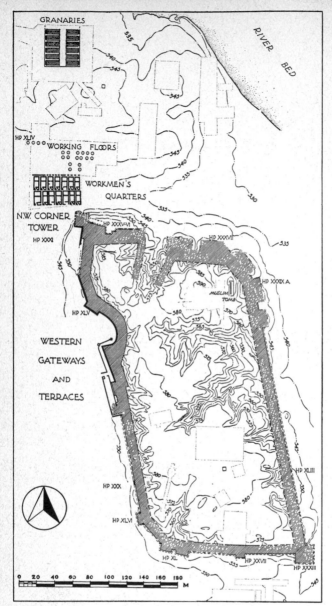

GRANARIES

RIVER BED

HP XLIV
WORKING FLOORS

WORKMEN'S
QUARTERS

N.W. CORNER
TOWER
HP XXXI

HP XXXV-VI

HP XXXVII

HP XXXIX A

HP XLV

MUSLIM
TOMB

WESTERN

GATEWAYS

AND

TERRACES

HP XLIII

HP XXX

HP XLVI

HP XL   HP XXVII   HP XXXII

0 20 40 60 80 100 120 140 160 180
M

29 The citadel of Harappā was plundered for its bricks for use in modern railway construction, but enough of its plan remains to show the thick citadel-walls of mud brick revetted with baked brick. To the north are the granaries reconstructed in *Ill. 32*. Within the citadel no recognizable buildings have survived

citadel, suggests close administrative control of the municipal food-stocks within convenient proximity to the river-highway. To the south of the citadel was an extensive cemetery of which more will be said.

At the time of writing (1965), the principal Indus site under excavation (by B.B. Lal and B.K. Thapar) is that

Ills. 34–37

30, 31 The fortification of the citadel mound at Harappā consisted of a revetted mud-brick rampart which was built on a base 40 ft wide. From this base it tapered upward. The revetment, of baked brick, shows work of at least two periods (*Ill. 30*). Behind the fortification a high mud platform carried the buildings of the interior as shown in the section (*Ill. 31* right)

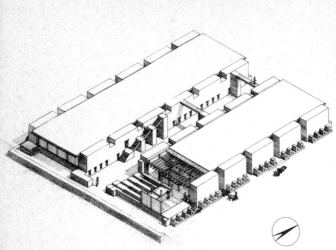

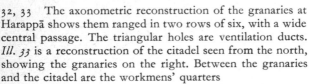

32, 33 The axonometric reconstruction of the granaries at Harappā shows them ranged in two rows of six, with a wide central passage. The triangular holes are ventilation ducts. *Ill. 33* is a reconstruction of the citadel seen from the north, showing the granaries on the right. Between the granaries and the citadel are the workmens' quarters

of Kalibangan, overlooking the dry valley of the river Ghaggar (former Sarasvatī) in the district of Ganganagar, Rajasthan, 100 miles south-east of Harappā. The visible vestiges comprise two mounds, a smaller towards the west and a larger towards the east. The former has at its base a pre-Harappan culture (see p. 32), which merges into the subsequent Harappan remains. These include a mud-brick platform, or accumulation of platforms, contained within an oblong frame of mud-brick walling armed with rectangular bastions; there was apparently an entrance with some baked brickwork on the southern side. Surviving samples show that externally the mud-brick construction was smoothed to a battered face with a coating of mud plaster.

Ill. 37

The purpose of this towered walling can scarcely have been other than defensive or, if itself purely formal, derived from a military prototype. A suggestion that it may have been designed to protect a ritual mound from

34 A view of two streets with houses at Kalibangan, one of the latest sites of the Indus Valley Civilization to be excavated. The neat geometrical plan should be noted (*cf. Ill. 14*)

river-floods is ruled out by the material used. (To defy a
flood with mud brick would be like defying it with
porridge!) No, the western mound of Kalibangan was a
Ill. 37
true citadel or the simulacrum of a true citadel, utilizing
a pre-existing mound as a convenient basis and matching
the walled mounds on the western flanks of Harappā and
Mohenjo-daro.

The eastern and lower mound of Kalibangan shows the
Harappan culture from the outset. It is an unfortified
town of modest size with street-plan of the grid type
oriented approximately on the cardinal points. Courtyard
Ill. 34
houses of baked and mud brick are associated with drains
of baked brick and the normal Harappan equipment, in
five successive stages. Towards the south-west of the two
mounds a cemetery has been identified, with typical
Ill. 36
Harappan burials – north–south, head to the north, and
with abundant grave-pottery. In one way and another, it
would appear that on lesser as on major Indus sites something approaching a standard urban layout is gradually
emerging: citadel, lower town, and inhumation-cemetery

35-37 The new site of Kalibangan has produced much evidence of the Harappan culture. The burials (*Ill. 36*, left) are typically Harappan, orientated with the head to the north and having abundant grave-goods, mainly pottery. The citadel had a defensive wall of which the exterior was smoothed with mud-plaster (*Ill. 35*). Strong rectangular mud-brick bastions stand out from it (*Ill. 37*). The defences characterize the western of the two mounds at Kalibangan

adjacent to the citadel. Naturally, variations may also be expected, particularly on small sites.

A smaller Harappan town has been partially excavated at Chanhu-daro, some 80 miles south of Mohenjo-daro. It apparently lacks the citadel of the larger cities but otherwise conforms to type in the use of drains, baked-brick houses and mud-brick platforms built in the recurrent endeavour to surmount the rising flood-level. Another small town, at Lothal on the sea-plain of Kāthiāwād 450 miles south-east of Mohenjo-daro, presents more individual features. The site, or at least a part of it which is now recognized as an 'acropolis', was raised and bolstered with mud brick and mud, but there was also a 'lower town'. Mud brick was used, as at Kalibangan, with baked brick in the main structure of the houses, though baths, drains, wells and, of course, kilns were throughout of baked brick and of normal Indus type. A substructure on the 'acropolis', with criss-cross ducts between a series of mud-brick blocks, each 12 ft square, is probably the basis of a granary similar in principle to that of Mohenjo-

Ills. 95, 96

33

38 The dock at Lothal is a major feature of this 'Saurashtrian Indus' site. Its sides are revetted in baked brick and at the lower end of the illustration can be seen the top of a well-constructed sluice-gate

Ill. 38

daro. It had been accidentally burnt, and baked sealings, presumably from bales stored at one time in the overlying barn, had fallen into the ducts. Near by, on a flank of the mound, a remarkable oblong enclosure 710 ft long and about 120 ft wide, with sides revetted in baked brick, has been identified as a dock for shipping. Further reference will be made to Lothal at a later stage.

These examples will serve to illustrate the general character of the Indus towns. Their surviving architecture is plain in the extreme, but the possibility or even likelihood of elaboration in timber, which has nowhere survived above the former ground-level, will present itself to anyone familiar with the rich Indian tradition in this material.

Inhabitants: Arts and Crafts

No 'royal tomb' has yet been identified in the Indus Civilization, an omission which is no doubt due to successive coverings of alluvium and to the incompleteness

39, 40 These two burials are from cemetery R37 at Harappā. Above, the corpse has been laid in an oblong grave revetted with mud brick. Right, the body was laid in a wooden coffin, traces of which may be seen as a faint outline round the skeleton. The provision of the numerous pots as grave-goods is typical of Indus Civilization burials (cf. Ill. 36)

of archaeological investigation. But at Harappā a graveyard manifestly of ordinary citizens has been partially exposed to the south of the citadel, and some sixty skeletons have been recovered from it. They were normally extended with the head towards the north, and each was accompanied by an average of fifteen or twenty pots representing the mature Indus culture. One of the graves had been revetted, on an oblong plan, with mud brick. In another, the body had been enclosed in a coffin of

Ill. 39
Ill. 40

which the side-walls had been of local rosewood (a scented timber) and the lid of deodar or cedar, doubtless floated down from the hills.

The anthropologists who have described these skeletons affirm that, so far as the evidence goes, the population of the Indus valley would appear to have remained more or less stable in character from Harappan times to the present day. In other words, the invasions of these regions which have certainly occurred at intervals throughout the last four thousand years must have been of similar human types or at any rate on too small a scale to bring about marked changes in physical characters. A long-headed (dolichocephalic) type predominates, generally comparable with the 'Proto-Australoid', 'Caucasic' or 'Eurafrican' of earlier writers; others, of slighter build, recall the conventional 'Mediterranean,' 'Indo-European' or 'Caspian' types of the anthropometric jargon. In height, the adults tended to range from 5 ft 5 ins to 5 ft 8–9 ins; and, what is of greater interest, the age at death fell mostly between twenty and forty, with a bias towards thirty. In view of the fact that adults only are included in this calculation, the expectation of life in the Indus Civilization, for all its fine houses and its drains, was low indeed.

More recently, at Lothal a number of burials (seventeen graves are mentioned) have been discovered high up on the north-western fringe of the site, belonging apparently to a late phase of the Indus Civilization. As at Harappā, most of the skeletons were oriented north-south, with the head towards the north, and the graves were occasionally lined with mud bricks. Three of the graves enclosed a double burial, possibly that of a man and a woman, though whether the Hindu custom of widow-sacrifice is indicated it is too early to say. The skulls which have been examined are reported to be on the average round-headed (brachycephalic) or at least mesocephalic, unlike the average at Harappā, but conforming with the average of the present

41, 42 Round seals with pierced projections at the back have been found on the islands of Bahrein and Failaka in the Persian Gulf. An example of one of these, above, is illustrated with an example of a similar type of seal from Mohenjo-daro on the right. Both are inscribed with a bull pictogram

inhabitants of Gujarat. Once more, a notable measure of continuity is suggested. No analysis of the skulls from the Kalibangan cemetery is yet available.

Amongst the equipment of the Indus citizens, priority must be given to their famous seals, generally of steatite, which are distinctive in kind and unique in quality. The normal seal was square with sides from $\frac{3}{4}$ to $1\frac{1}{4}$ ins and with a perforated boss at the back for handling and suspension. Exceptionally the seal is round, with or without a boss, and there are a few cylinder seals reminiscent of those of Mesopotamia; but the essential individuality of the Indus seals is emphasized by contrast with more or less remote analogies, mostly circular with a pierced boss, found in southern Mesopotamia and on islands (Failaka and Bahrein) in the Persian Gulf and representing a north-westerly extension of Indus influence transmuted by the alien commercial world of those regions.

Ills. 41, 42

Carved on the Indus seals with a small chisel and a drill are intaglio designs (*i.e.* engraved with a sunk pattern, so that the impression appears in relief) which may often be claimed as small masterpieces. They include a wide range of animals which must clearly have been at that time familiar denizens of the Indus valley: elephant, tiger, rhinoceros, antelope, crocodile or gharial. Above all, the zebu or humped bull is majestically rendered, with a monumental strength out of all proportion to the small field available. The commonest type is that of an ox-like

Ills. 43, 44

43 A wide range of subjects, mainly animals, is shown on Indus seals. Noteworthy are the three seals in the upper row showing a fine rhinoceros, a zebu or humped bull, and an elephant which apparently wears a back-cloth, presumably indicating domestication. The curious human figure in the centre of the lower row appears to represent a prototype of the god Śiva

44 The ox-like beast shown on this steatite pectoral has been nicknamed the 'unicorn', but its apparently single horn may merely be a convention intended to illustrate one horn behind the other. The 'unicorn' is the commonest representation found on Indus seals and is invariably shown with a short post before the animal. This may be a decorative manger or even an incense-burner. There are many variations in the style in which this strange object is rendered and certain identification is difficult. The illustration shows the pectoral twice actual size

beast seemingly with a single horn and nicknamed there-fore the 'unicorn'; it may be suspected that two horns are in fact intended, one behind the other, but it has been recalled that Ktesias and Aristotle both ascribed the unicorn to India. In front of the 'unicorn' is invariably a strange object on a short post, commonly if grotesquely

Ill. 44

named a 'standard', but possibly representing a decorative manger, or even an incense-burner. Composite grotesque animals also occur; one has the face of a man, the trunk and tusks of an elephant, the horns of a bull, the forepart of a ram, and the hindquarters of a tiger with erect tail armed with claws. Sometimes human forms are included, though the inferiority of their rendering recalls a similar disparity between the human and animal figures of the palaeolithic cave-art of western Europe. Three examples from Mohenjo-daro have a special interest in that they appear to represent a prototype of the great god Śiva of the later Hindu religion.

Ill. 43

Most of the seals bear also a short inscription in a pictographic script which, in spite of brave attempts, has not yet been interpreted. The pictographs are as different from those of Mesopotamia and Egypt as are these from each other. It is an interesting phenomenon that, within a short range of time and space, three great civilizations produced three utterly divergent systems of notation. The possible significance of this fact will be considered later.

The full function of these seals – more than 1200 of them have been found at Mohenjo-daro alone – remains uncertain until their inscriptions are understood. They were used (as at Lothal, see above) to stamp clay sealings on bales and other commodities, and it is likely therefore that, in part at any rate, they represent personal names. The scarcity of duplicate inscriptions is a difficulty, but at least seems to rule out a religious or descriptive connotation. The boss or handle pierced for a cord implies that the seals were normally carried by their owners; and a fair measure of literacy in the Indus population is to be inferred also from the recurrence of the script as graffiti on pots or potsherds.

Of Indus stone sculpture, only eleven more or less fragmentary examples from Mohenjo-daro and two doubt-

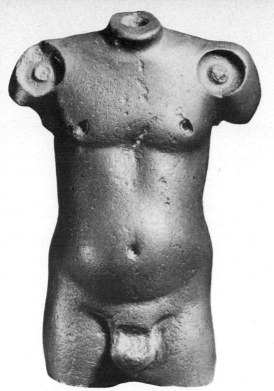

45, 46 These two stone torsos from Harappā are masterpieces of miniature modelling. The example on the left is of red stone and that on the right grey stone. In both cases the head and arms were made separately and fitted into sockets, and the right-hand figure was ithyphallic. These torsos may (or may not) be of later date than the Indus Civilization

ful (possibly later) torsos from Harappā are at present known. All are of small size; save for two animals, of which one was a composite ram-elephant, they represent men or gods, four or five of them in squatting attitude. The heads are characterized by an extreme disharmony of the face in relation to the low receding forehead, by narrow but not Mongoloid eyes, and by the gathering of the hair in a 'bun' at the back. A beard is worn, but the upper lip is shaven, and the eyes are (or were) inlaid with shell; in these respects there is a resemblance with approximately contemporary heads from Mesopotamia and eastern Syria (*e.g.* at Tell Asmar and Mari), but otherwise the owl-like stare of the Mesopotamian type is widely different from the more contemplative aspect of the Indus

Ills. 45, 46

Ill. 48

Ills. 49, 50

Ills. 47, 51

47–51 Few examples of Indus stone sculpture survive. *Ills.* *47* and *51* possibly represent a 'priest-king' or deity. The domineering aspect of the face contrasts with the more humane aspect of the head below, *Ills.* *49*, *50*, which is far pleasanter. Both heads share the trimmed beard, shaven upper lip and fillet around the head, and have a low receding forehead with the hair gathered behind in a bun. *Ill.* *48*, above right, is a terracotta figurine of a squatting man, or possibly a monkey, which is almost verging upon the style of the grotesques found at Mohenjo-daro (*cf. Ill. 61*)

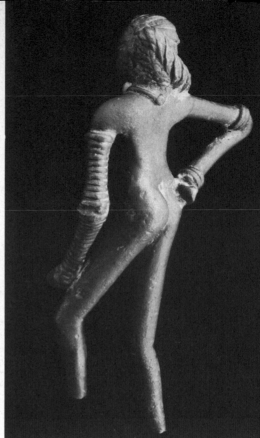

52, 53 This bronze dancing girl is the most remarkable of the Indus figurines. Pert and provocative, she is naked except for her necklace and her many bangles. Her entire attitude is one of assurance and her head, expressively tilted, is a skilful impression of an 'aboriginal' type

faces. There is indeed nothing significantly in common between the sculptures of the two regions. In bronze only a few minor works have survived; notably, a life-like figurine of a buffalo with swept-back horns, and a statuette *Ills. 52, 53* of a pert and provocative dancing-girl, naked except for an abundance of armlets. Of small terracottas there is a *Ill. 57* great abundance, including countless oxen and buffaloes, sometimes rendered with force and expressiveness but more often merely pedestrian trade-goods. Human terra-*Ills. 54, 55* cotta figurines normally represent women wearing only abundant jewellery and, sometimes, bizarre 'pannier' *Ills. 61, 63, 64* head-dresses. There are also occasional comic figures of

44

54, 55 In contrast to the dancing girl opposite, the terracotta figurines of women, or 'mother goddesses', are grotesquely over-dressed with heavy jewellery although they otherwise apparently wear only skimpy skirts and occasionally bizarre 'pannier' head-dresses

58–60 A terracotta hen, dove and cat (or tiger) were probably toys but may possibly have been votive figurines

56, 57, 62 The modern bullock-cart from Sind shown above has changed little since the terra-cotta model of a similar cart, opposite left, was made at Mohenjo-daro. The terracotta bull and buffalo, shown half actual size are similarly very faithful reproductions of their modern counter-parts and the bull in fact enjoyed a precedence among the terracottas found

61, 63, 64 The makers of terracottas at Mohenjo-daro enjoyed a sense of humour, shown by numerous grotesque figurines. *Ill. 61*, opposite right, shows a curious human figure apparently with its tongue lolling out. *Ill. 63*, below left, is seemingly a caricature of a fat woman and *Ill. 64*, right, shows a strange 'flook-like' creature hiding its eyes or hugging its muzzle

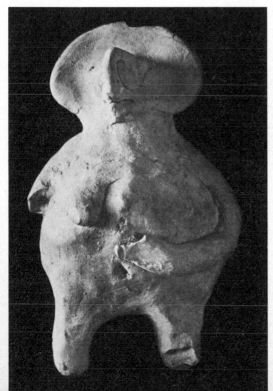

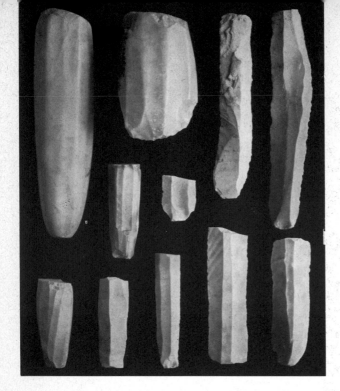

65, 66 Parallel-sided chert flakes were struck from a prepared core, often without retouch. Some of the cores were then used as burnishers. *Ill. 66*, above, are examples of copper fish-hooks. Nearly actual size

Ills. 56, 62

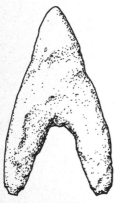

67 Copper arrowhead from Mohenjo-daro

a human or animal character, and toy carts with solid wheels, usually of terracotta but rarely of copper or bronze, are common enough. Of all these products, a majority were probably toys, but some of them – female figures and perhaps bulls – may be thought to have been votive. It may be observed that bulls are represented but not cows, hens but not cocks; evidently the draught-bull and the egg-producing hen enjoyed a proper precedence, as did the mother or mother-goddess emblem of fertility.

Important contrasts between the Indus and the Meso-potamian cultures have already been noted, but none is more striking than that exhibited by the tool-types of the two regions. Throughout the Indus Civilization the common domestic implement was a parallel-sided chert blade struck from a prepared core, more often than not without retouch. The cores themselves often show a high polish from their secondary use as burnishers. Stone mace-heads also occur, though examples of copper or

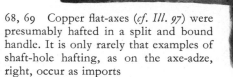

68, 69   Copper flat-axes (*cf. Ill. 97*) were presumably hafted in a split and bound handle. It is only rarely that examples of shaft-hole hafting, as on the axe-adze, right, occur as imports

bronze were not unknown. Copper-bronze implements include spears, knives, short swords, arrowheads, axes and fish-hooks. The spearheads are tanged and cannot clearly be distinguished from knives, though knives are sometimes differentiated from spears by a slightly sinuous recurved point, a peculiarity hardly ever found outside the Indus Civilization. The thinness of all these blades is remarkable, and seems to demand some special stiffening by being set well back between the split ends of the shaft or handle. The axes are flat, without shaft-hole, and were presumably hafted in a split and bound handle. Some of them are long and narrow, with nearly parallel sides; others are short and relatively wide, with boldly expanded edge. The obstinate retention of this primitive type long after the shaft-hole had been developed in western Asia (as early as the 'Ubaid period before 3000 BC in Meso-potamia) is the more remarkable in that examples of this superior method of hafting did on rare occasions reach

Ill. 66

Ill. 68

Ill. 69

49

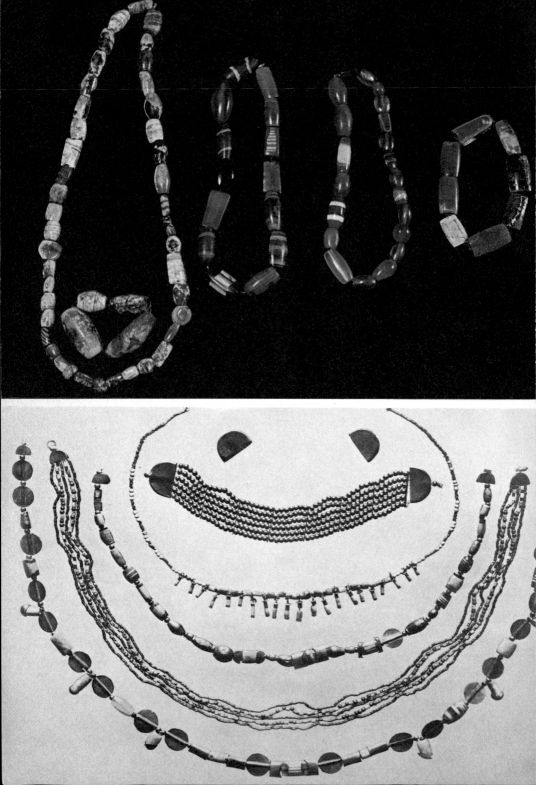

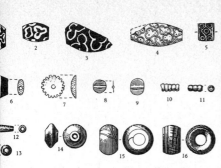

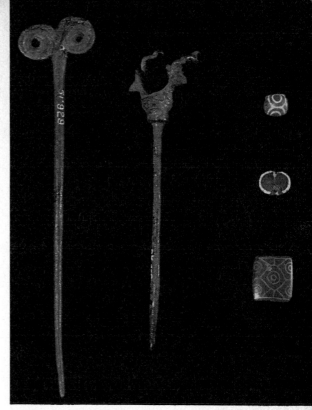

70–73 The beads and jewellery from many Indus sites show distinct links with the ancient civilizations of the West. Faience segmented beads occur in northern Syria, Crete and Egypt between 3000 and 1500 BC: etched carnelian beads are found at Ur, Kish and Tell Asmar (about 2300 BC), and gold beads from Mohenjo-daro may be paralleled in Mesopotamia about 2400–2300 BC and at Troy IIG about 2300 BC. Examples of all these types of beads are illustrated here. The bronze pins in *Ill. 73* are from Mohenjo-daro

the Indus. Copper seems never whole-heartedly to have occupied the genius of the Indus craftsmen; as a relatively costly import, it was used with economy, although, in addition to implements, bowls, cups and dishes were sometimes made of the material. The ore may have been obtained overland from Rajasthan or from Afghanistan, but supplementary imports by sea may be suspected, and tin was almost certainly introduced in this manner.

Unlike these utile products, beads do show a few clear links with the West and help thus to mitigate the isolation of the Indus culture. Circular beads of gold with a prominent axial tube occur at Mohenjo-daro, in Mesopotamia about 2400–2300 BC, and in Troy 11 G about 2300 BC, whilst faïence copies from the Indus are likely to be

Ills. 70–73

home-made. Again, 'segmented' faïence beads are numerous in the Indus and occur between 3000 and 1500 BC in northern Syria, Crete and Egypt. Etched carnelian beads are identical at Mohenjo-daro, Chanhu-daro, and in Mesopotamia at Ur, Kish and Tell Asmar (about 2300 BC). Other types are more local, but they include a distinctive trefoil decoration (perhaps of astral significance) which is found also on one of the Mohenjo-daro sculptures and a stone base and on stone, pottery and woodwork in Mesopotamia, Crete and Egypt between 2300 and 1300 BC. The Indus Civilization provides a clear – though not the only – instance of an interchange of ornaments and charms (or their forms) combined with a basic technological independence.

Ills. 72, 73

Ills. 47, 51

Lastly, the pottery. Most of the Indus pots are wheel-turned and are of pinkish ware with a bright red slip, though a buff background is not uncommon. Decoration, normally in black, consists either of plain horizontal lines of varying thickness, or of more pictorial motifs; notably, intersecting circles, scale-patterns, chequers, pipal leaves, rosettes, lattice-work, cross-hatching, and occasional peacocks and fish. Human figures are very rare and are relatively crude. Shapes include 'dish on stand' or fruit-dish (an Asian type widespread in time and space), small vessels bearing a knobbed decoration, large slender-footed bowls or containers, cylindrical perforated strainers, and cream-coloured goblets with pointed foot. The last are sometimes stamped with lettering, presumably the potter's name, and are confined to the late period in the Indus valley itself; the more southerly extensions of the Civilization in Kāthiāwād (or Saurashtra) do not seem to have used the type, and on the other hand it is absent from pre- or non-Indus settlements in the Indus and neighbouring regions.

Ills. 74–77

Ill. 76

The general impression given by the Indus pottery is that of efficient mass-production.

74, 75 Indus pots are often of fine quality and are mostly wheel-turned. Their decoration is normally in black, and ranges from plain horizontal lines through a variety of more pictorial motifs. The jar, *Ill. 74*, right, comes from cemetery R37 at Harappā and its colours include buff, pink, red and black. The group of peacocks in addition to the various leaf motifs should be noted. *Ill. 75*, below, shows a vase and a plate from the post-Indus cemetery H at Harappā. Here the close-filling style of decoration of *Ill. 74* is missing and a more open variety favoured. The examples show a peacock on the vase and a gazelle (?) with curiously waved horns on the plate

76 A number of cream-coloured goblets with a pointed foot have been found with lettering stamped upon them. This stamp is presumably a potter's mark; the goblets occur in late Indus contexts. The example shown comes from Harappā

77 Two fragments of pottery of an exceptional ▷ type, with animal motifs, from Mohenjo-daro (opposite) show attractive colouring in red and buff

Pre-Indus Cultures

For the material ancestry of the Indus Civilization a systematic search is still necessary and would not indeed be difficult to organize. Thus the high mound of Dābar Kot in the Zhob valley of northern Baluchistan exhibits in its sides the Indus Culture bracketed above and below by other cultures, and would amply reward a single season's excavation carried out with skill and purpose. Or the considerable Indus site of Judeirjo-daro recently noted on the plain 18 miles north of Jacobabad in Sind, with its superficial hint of a relatively early date, would doubtless provide a new and valuable introductory phase to our problem. Meanwhile, four sites may be singled out as of special interest in this context.

The first is Amrī, 100 miles south of Mohenjo-daro in Sind. There, over an area of some 20 acres, are mounds formerly continuous but long divided and eroded by floods from the adjacent Indus. The importance of the site

as containing a Harappan (Indus Valley) culture superimposed upon an earlier, so-called 'Amri', culture was
recognized in 1929 and led to intensive excavation by
J.-M. Casal in 1959–62. Both cultures were Chalcolithic;
fragments of copper or bronze were present from the outset and slightly increased in quantity as time went by, but
either metal was never abundant or it has largely perished.
Blades and cores of chert continued in use throughout.

The 'Amri' culture fell into four phases (A–D), of
which the two later were marked by mud-brick structures
consisting of numerous small, doorless compartments,
presumably intended merely as basements. The pottery
was at first largely hand-made, but the use of the wheel
increased as the culture developed. The better and more
characteristic wares are of buff, cream or pink colour,
usually with a plain band of reddish brown at the neck
and with a geometric design in black or chocolate giving
a polychromatic effect to the whole. The patterns, painted

apparently after firing, include panels of chequer-work or hatching, chevrons, lozenges and zigzags or 'sigmas'. Only at the end of the period do animal forms appear, but these occasionally have a schematic liveliness, as in a scene of caprids with a dog or wolf. More usually a stylized bull suffices, commonly painted in brown on a yellowish surface.

Ill. 79

In no significant respect does this 'Amri' pottery anticipate that of the Indus Civilization, but equally there is no hint that it long preceded it. Its distribution lies primarily between the Indus river and the southern Baluch hills, but it is related to that of variant cultures in the hills themselves, between Quetta and the sea. At the end of the phase there is a slight intrusion of forms associated with the Harappan culture. This Harappan admixture becomes more noticeable in the succeeding 'Intermediate' phase, and coincides with a shrinkage in the area of occupation and evidences of general decline. The inference is that the Harappans were spreading into the region and building rival towns of their own; as at Chanhu-daro, less than 30 miles eastward across the Indus.

At the same time a number of sherds show animal-representations similar to those of the Kulli culture of southern Baluchistan. This culture was partly contemporary with Harappā and Mohenjo-daro (for example at Nindowari, north of Bela), and offers another useful link amongst the miscellaneous industries of this complex age.

The decline of Amri continued throughout its main Harappan period and its succeeding 'Jhukar' and 'Jhangar' periods which will be referred to later (p. 84). As a whole, the story of Amri prepares us for evidence which is now emerging from other sites. The famous Indus Valley Civilization was not an immediately omnivorous phenomenon, in the the Valley itself or elsewhere. In terms of chronology, the appearance and duration of a minor town of the Indus complex may well have little

78 These potsherds were found in excavations beneath the citadel-defences at Harappā. They are important evidence for a pre-Indus culture and are similar in their decoration of finely ruled horizontal black lines to pottery from sites in northern Baluchistan and at Kot Diji

bearing upon the appearance and duration of Mohenjo-daro or Harappā. Differential elements surviving to the present day offer a warning; village-industries not infrequently linger on in the face of central mass-production. Certainly Carbon-14 dates from sites such as Lothal or Kalibangan may fail significantly to define the terminal dates of the Civilization in its metropolitan manifestations.

The second of the four selected sites is Harappā itself. There in 1946 slight traces of a pre-Indus culture were found beneath the citadel-defences, which here marked the arrival of the Indus Civilization. These traces are restricted to potsherds of a fine dark purple-red ware decorated, particularly round the rim, with carefully ruled horizontal black bands. This ware recalls other non-Indus wares at Kot Diji and Kalibangan (see pp. 58 and 60) and in northern Baluchistan, but has no close affinity with those of the mature Indus Civilization.

Ill. 78

79 These three pots, of the so-called 'Nal' type, were found in Baluchistan. Although this type of pottery pre-dates Indus ware it is in no way ancestral to the pottery of the Indus Civilization

The third site is the most striking of the four. At Kot Diji, 25 miles north-east of Mohenjo-daro, exploration by F. A. Khan has revealed a fortified village – or small town with a fortified citadel – beneath an open Indus settlement. The site showed sixteen layers of occupation of which the last three were typical of the Indus Civilization, the fourth was 'mixed', and the remainder represented an antecedent culture that has been called specifically 'Kot Dijian'. Based on a 'half life' of 5730 years, the Carbon-14 dating for a late Kot Dijian stratum (4A from the top) is understood to be 2100 BC±140 years, and for Layer 14 (the lowest but two) 2600 BC±145 years. The late date for Kot Dijian 4A immediately prior to full Harappan, if verified by further samples, certainly implies that the Kot Dijian culture continued long after the first arrival of the Harappan or Indus Valley culture in the vicinity. Harappan elements, such as the typically Harappan scale-pattern, in the Kot Dijian levels are consistent with this prolonged overlap. Once more we have a differential development and time-scale as between the metropolitan and contemporary provincial sites.

The open settlement of the top three layers is marked by characteristic Indus pottery, including pierced strainers and sherds showing intersecting-circle, pipal-leaf, comb, and scale decoration, in black on red. Between it and the underlying Kot Dijian was a burnt layer, thought to represent the destruction of the earlier settlement with its fortification of mud brick on stone foundations. The house-walls throughout were similarly built of mud-brick on lower courses of stone; baked bricks do not seem to have been used at all. Copper or bronze occurred in the uppermost (Indus) levels but were absent from the Kot Dijian occupation, which produced chert blades and cores and leaf-shaped chert arrowheads such as are otherwise rare in the Baluch-Indus region. The Kot Dijian pottery is wheel-turned, light and thin, is pinkish to red in colour, and is commonly decorated in black with straight horizontal lines or sometimes with waves and loops; it bears a marked similarity to the pre-citadel pottery at Harappā and to some of the Amrī wares. But in two respects this Kot Dijian culture anticipates or overlaps that of the Indus Civilization. First, its pottery

Ill. 24

already includes vessels decorated with the peculiarly Indus scale-pattern; and secondly, it also contains some of the strange triangular terracotta 'cakes' ($1\frac{1}{2}$ to 4 ins across) which are not otherwise known outside the Indus Civilization. These 'cakes' have been vaguely regarded as ritual objects, but their frequent occurrence in drains suggests a toilet use. Be that as it may, a link between the Kot Dijians and the Indus folk is indicated, though the significance of that link remains in doubt. As a whole, the Kot Dijian culture can scarcely claim to have been in any direct sense parental to that of the Indus cities. Rather would it appear to have been a partially antecedent, partially overlapping provincial culture which was eventually brought sharply within the orbit of Mohenjo-daro. In this respect the evidence of Kot Diji repeats that of Amrī (see p. 56).

Ills. 34–37

The fourth site is that of Kalibangan in northern Rajasthan, under excavation since 1961. At the base of the western mound of this site has been found a pre-Harappan or proto-Harappan chalcolithic culture marked by mud brick (no baked brick) buildings and by a ceramic mainly of an unslipped dull red fabric with black bands having subjoined loops round the neck or supplemented by fronds or hatched segments or triangles. Some resemblance has been recognized with the pre-Harappan or non-Harappan pottery both of Kot Diji and of Harappā itself, but its relationship (if any) with that of the Indus Civilization is still speculative.

Without further argument, then, it may be affirmed that the immediate material origins of the Indus Civilization in the narrower aspects of art and craftsmanship cannot at present be demonstrated. But what of the wider aspects of the matter? Here factors of a less material and proportionately more speculative character cannot be avoided if our essay is to be something more than a catalogue.

Early Settlers in the Indus Valley

First, let it be emphasized that to the venturous mind the wide plains of the Indus valley offered a lure and a challenge. They were at that time in some measure marsh- and jungle-ridden, the haunt of the noxious beasts which were later to adorn the Indus seals, and of the fevers which modern science is at last eliminating. But they were widely fertile, and their fertility was renewed by annual floods, whilst the great rivers, full of edible fish, were also natural highways between the mountains and the sea. With this expansive prospect, any imaginative spirit, oppressed by the claustrophobia of his mountain retreat, may well have felt the stirrings of ambition. Yet ambition alone would not carry him far. The great rivers, for all their beneficence, were at the same time treacherous and formidable enemies. If not constrained and directed by wise, large-scale and sustained effort, they were destroyers no less than fertilizers, as anyone who has seen a great river in turbulent flood will testify. A society determined to profit by the vast opportunities of the plain must needs have also the genius and the skill to master an exacting and minatory environment, *and must have it from the outset*. A civilization such as that of the Indus cannot be visualized as a slow and patient growth. Its victories, like its problems, must have been of a sudden sort; and our search therefore for a systematic material ancestry for the Indus Civilization may well be a long and subtle and perhaps not primarily important one.

Intellectually, the founders of that Civilization had one crowning advantage. Two great riverine civilizations had shortly preceded them, in Mesopotamia and in Egypt. In any physical sense, neither of these was the immediate parent; the Indus Civilization, with its individual technology and script and its alien personality, was no mere colony of the West. But ideas have wings, and in the third millennium the *idea* of civilization was in the *air* of

Ill. 80

western Asia. A model of civilization, however abstract, was present to the minds of the Indus founders. In their running battle against more spacious problems than had been encountered either in Mesopotamia or in Egypt, they were fortified by the consciousness that *it, or something like it, had been done before*. And in that consciousness, after one failure and another (Amrī and Kot Diji are merely examples), they won through.

In some such manner may be reconstructed the initial phase of the Indus Civilization: as the ultimate triumph of a village or small-town community, determined, well led and inspired by a great and mature idea. The Indus people were neither the first nor the last to fulfil themselves in this dramatic fashion; and it is a fashion not easy to reconstruct on the limited basis of conventional archaeological evidence. It is not necessarily the less objectively true for that disability, for the abstract element in its composition.

Expansion and Economy of the Indus Civilization

Ills. 1, 2

At one stage or another of its career, the range of the Indus Civilization was of astonishing extent. On what may be called the Indus axis it extended for 1000 miles from Sutkāgen Dor near the shores of the Arabian Sea 300 miles west of Karachi to the neighbourhood of Rupar at the foot of the Simla hills. South-eastwards along the coast exploration in recent years has shown that it stretched for more than 425 miles from Karachi, through Kāthiā-wāḍ or Saurashtra to the estuaries of the Narbadā and the Kim on the Gulf of Cambay; and this new coastal spread has introduced new and important elements, both cultural and chronological, into the Indus problem. Nor do the new factors end there. In 1958 definite evidence was found for the first time that the Indus culture, including the characteristic triangular terracotta 'cakes', had leapt or circumvented the barriers of desert and jungle which had

Ill. 24

80 The great rivers of the Indus Valley have always been a source of food as well as great highways. Flat-bottomed boats of the type used today for fishing in the Indus in all probability illustrate their ancestral counterparts, although of these very little evidence has survived

previously been thought to exclude the Civilization from the Yamunā or Jumna basin, and had reached Alamgirpur, near a tributary of that river 17 miles west of Meerut and only 28 miles north-east of Delhi. A further report that Indus pottery has been found under the ancient metropolis of Kaushāmbi, much lower down the Yamunā, is not confirmed, but a fringe of Indus or sub-Indus sites must now be expected on the northern plains. Within the past dozen years the pattern of the Indus Civilization has been materially enlarged and significantly changed.

How did the great Civilization make its living? First and foremost, like its older contemporaries in Mesopotamia and Egypt, by farming. Wheat and six-rowed barley were grown, and field-peas; melon seeds, sesame and a few date-stones have also been found, and the earliest traces of cotton known anywhere in the world. There may have been rice, though evidence for this (at Lothal) is at present slight. Domestic animals included dogs and cats, humped cattle, short-horns and buffaloes, and possibly pigs, camels, horses and asses – perhaps too the elephant, though the identification of a back-cloth in representations of this animal on Indus seals is the only evidence and is less than certain. But whether the elephant was or was not tamed, its ivory was freely used.

Ill. 43

Next to agriculture, trade. Apart from overland caravans, which may be assumed, the long coastline and arterial rivers now known to have been contained within the Indus territories are consistent with an appreciable domestic and international trafficking by water. Archaeology and geology show that imports included gold from southern India or Afghanistan, copper from Rajasthan or Afghanistan or even farther afield, lapis lazuli from Afghanistan, turquoise from Iran, and a jade-like fuchsite probably from southern India. Links with Mesopotamia have already been noted, and may be extended to include Indus pottery and inlays from Akkadian levels (*c.* 2300 BC) at Tell Asmar. There was certainly also a traffic in perishable objects, notably wood. But whether this western (Persian Gulf) trade can be further localized from written record is matter for discussion. Sumerian and Akkadian cuneiform documents refer to a land called Dilmun or Telmun, which was regarded as an otherworldly paradise, a place 'where the sun rises' and therefore somewhere to the east of Sumer; it was also a substantial source of material goods. Thus ships of Dilmun brought timber to Ur-Nanshe of Lagash about 2450 BC, and the great Sargon about a century later records that shipping from Dilmun, Magan and Meluhha docked in his new capital Agade. (The site of Agade has not been

81 This steatite circular seal, found during recent excavations at Lothal, is neither wholly Indian nor Sumerian in its design. It is of the type known as 'Persian Gulf' seals which appear to have been made at various entrepôts, notably Bahrein, for the Persian Gulf trade (*cf. Ills. 41, 42*)

identified, though M. E. L. Mallowan has suggested the neighbourhood of Babylon). Other documents show that in the twentieth century B C seafarers were bringing to Ur, in southern Mesopotamia, gold, silver, much copper, lumps of lapis lazuli, stone beads, ivory combs and ornaments and inlays, eye-paint, wood, and perhaps pearls ('fish-eyes'). Dilmun has commonly been identified with the island of Bahrein, which must, if so, have been a revictualling and middleman station rather than a source. A. L. Oppenheim regards 'Meluhha' as the Indus valley and its civilization; S. N. Kramer prefers to identify Dilmun itself with the land of the Indus, and there are other views. But in one way or another the texts would appear to include reference to an organized trade between Sumeria and the Indus valley before and after 2000 B C.

A new appreciation of the length and development of the Indus seaboard fits in with this miscellaneous evidence for overseas commerce. Reference has already been made to the southerly port of Lothal, with its considerable dock, at the head of the Gulf of Cambay. It may well be no accident that Lothal has produced one of those strange circular seals of steatite, already mentioned, which are faintly reminiscent of Indus seals but were seemingly at home in the north-western half of the Persian Gulf (Bahrein, Failaka, southern Mesopotamia) about 1900 B C and have so been named specifically 'Persian Gulf seals'. More

Ill. 38

Ill. 81

recently a fresh examination of the Makran coast, on the northern flank of the Arabian Sea, has produced contributory evidence. In that very different environment, two sites – one of them new to knowledge – suggest a somewhat similar economic context. Here, 200–300 miles west of Karachi, geological and geographical evidence supports the probability that the ancient coastline was mostly much farther inland than it is today; and the two sites in question, now some miles from the coast, anciently commanded navigable estuaries within ready reach of the sea.

The first of these sites, Sutkāgen-dor, was discovered in 1876, but only in 1960 was it adequately placed upon the map. It lies on the eastern edge of the Dasht valley, now some 30 miles from the Arabian Sea. It consists of a formidable citadel and a lower, unfortified settlement of less certain extent; the former an oblong area nearly 580 ft in length by 340 ft in breadth, with a stone fortification-wall nearly 25 ft wide supplemented by an internal mud-brick platform 8 ft broad and indications of rectangular towers. In the southern wall was a narrow entrance, only 6 ft wide. The associated culture was almost entirely Harappan.

About 85 miles east of Sutkāgen Dor a similar site was identified for the first time above the Shadi Kaur valley, 8 miles north of Pasni. Apparently a fortified settlement here crowned an outcrop of rock, though details are lacking. The pottery was again mainly Harappan. The site is known as Sotka Koh, 'burnt hill'.

To these sites a third may probably be added: that of Bala Kot near Sonmiani, 45 miles north-west of Karachi, and now 12 miles from the receded coastline. This has not been explored, but the function of all three sites is scarcely in doubt. They imply two things: maritime traffic, and, at least in two cases, access to the hinterland up arterial valleys. As posting-stations on a long-range trade-route they make sense; in this cheerless countryside no merely local explanation is valid. No doubt others of their kind await discovery farther up this coast.

By and large, therefore, an appreciable commerce may be postulated between the civilization of the Tigris–Euphrates and that of the Indus. But be it repeated that this does not imply any close cultural integration between the two regions. Their interchange was, it seems, mostly restricted to goods of a secondary kind, of which the most important may well have been the ivory and the timber seemingly mentioned in the records. Whether Indus cotton should be added, the evidence is too slight to say.

The Date of the Indus Civilization

Until recent years our knowledge of the dating of the Indus Civilization was derived exclusively from contacts with western Asia and, more particularly, with Sumer and Akkad. Some of these have already been cited. On the current Mesopotamian chronology, they imply dates ranging from before 2350 BC to the seventeenth or sixteenth century BC, with a strong focus upon the Sargonid period which is now closely dated to 2370–2284 BC. The ends of the over-all bracket were, however, insecurely fixed by the contacts available; to cover them amply, I proposed in 1946 a period of *c.* 2500–1500 BC for the Civilization, without any emphasis on the exactitude of the terminal figures.

In 1949 the dating of ancient organic materials on the basis of their radio-carbon content (Carbon-14) introduced a new chronological datum into prehistoric or anhistoric archaeology, and, although errors and uncertainties remain in the method, supplied new controls which have widely, and perhaps on the whole fairly accurately, adjusted our perspective of the human achievement within the past 40,000 years. Upwards of a dozen of these radio-carbon or Carbon-14 dates are now available for the Indus Civilization; all except those for Kot Diji (from

Pennsylvania) are from the Tata Institute of Fundamental Research, Bombay.

First, the pre-Harappan 'Kot Diji' culture at Kot Diji, east of Mohenjo-daro:

(1) *Kot Diji*: from layer 14, the lowest 'Kot Dijian' layer but two on the site, 2605 BC ± 145 (on a 'half life' of 5730 ± 40); or 2471 BC ± 141 (on a 'half life' of 5568 ± 30).

From the latest 'Kot Dijian' layer (4A), beneath the Harappan, 2100 BC ± 138 ('half life' 5730) or 1975 BC ± 134 ('half life' 5568).

Two dates from 'Kot Dijian' layer 5 are 2250/2133 BC and 2330/2211 BC with similar margins.

Secondly from normal Harappan sites:

(2) *Kalibangan*: late (high) level of the Harappan culture: 1910 BC ± 105 ('half life' 5730) or 1790 BC ± 100 ('half life' 5568). On a 'middle' level, equivalent dates are: 1960 ± 105 or 1350 ± 100 BC; and 1930 ± 105 or 1825 ± 100 BC. On a 'lower middle' level, equivalent dates are: 2030 BC ± 105 or 1915 BC ± 100; and 2060 ± 105 BC or 1945 ± 100 BC.

(3) *Mohenjo-daro*: charred grains found long ago and ascribed to a late level: 1760 BC ± 115 ('half life' 5730) or 1650 BC ± 110 ('half life' 5568).

(4) *Lothal*: Harappan phases ('Lothal A') I–IV; 'sub-Harappan' ('Lothal B') phase V. Dates available are as follows:

Lothal A, phase IIIb (three samples): 2000–2010 BC ± 115 ('half life' 5730) or 1880–1895 BC ± 120 ('half life' 5568). Phase IVa: 1895 BC ± 115 ('half life' 5730) or 1790 BC ± 110 ('half life' 5568).

Lothal B, phase Va: 1800 BC ± 140 ('half life' 5730) or 1700 BC ± 135 ('half life' 5568). Another sample gave respectively 1865 BC or 1755 BC ± 110.

In estimating the values of these radio-carbon dates, certain sources of error have to be remembered. First, the samples analysed, even if correctly placed stratigraphically, are prone at various stages to contamination which may falsify their dating in serious measure. The available series is at present far too short to eliminate this risk; at least another fifty carefully selected analyses are required. Secondly, all the dates given are subject to margins of error varying from 200 to 282 years; a deterring possibility when the total period in question is a matter of merely a few centuries. Too often, the central date is hastily accepted as significant, with wholly inadequate allowance for the relatively wide range of alternatives. Thirdly, it is too easily assumed that 'early' samples represent the beginning of a culture, and that 'late' samples mark its end. The accident of either series being exactly or nearly terminal at either end of the bracket is sufficiently unlikely. All that can normally be inferred (after allowance for the margin of error already referred to) is that the culture was already in existence at the earlier terminal date, and that it survived the later. Fourthly – a point already stressed – the initial and final dates, if correctly diagnosed, of any particular Indus site cannot be applied without much further evidence to any other Indus site. The terminal dates of Harappā, for example, if we knew them, could not be applied blindly to Mohenjo-daro. Still less can the initial or terminal dates of Lothal or Kalibangan be applied to either of the metropolitan sites. The possibility of errors and disparities, from many causes, is thus almost infinite. At its best, in dealing with late prehistoric and early protohistoric cultures, we have to confess that radio-carbon analysis, a marvel for which we are properly grateful, is nevertheless a blunt instrument.

Of far greater precision is the witness of comparative archaeology in the relatively few instances where it is at present available. Both from archaeological and from epigraphical evidence, it is known that in the time of the great Sargon of Agade and his successors contact between southern Mesopotamia and the Indus was at its liveliest. And within a mere handful of years the date of Sargon is now securely established: as nearly as may be 2370–2344 BC; or, to take the Sargonid period as a whole, let us say 2370–2284 BC. Thereafter a second wave of Mesopotamian trade began with King Ur-Nammu, about 2100 BC, and continued until the Larsa period, about 1900 BC. Here is no dallying with margins of error between 200 and 300 years wide. Here is near-historical precision of a kind by which new material evidence from the Indus and Mesopotamia, and perhaps a new study of some of the old evidence, may be expected in the fullness of time to lend a fresh exactness to the dating of our Indus Civilization. Meanwhile, the occurrence of Indus seals in Sargonid associations at Ur, Kish and Tell Asmar; of etched beads, as used by the Harappans, from similar levels at Tell Asmar; of gold disk-beads with axial tube at Mohenjo-daro, at Early Dynastic III – Sargonid dates in Mesopotamia, and in Troy IIG about 2300 BC; and bone inlays and knobbed pottery of distinctively Indus types in Sargonid deposits at Tell Asmar; all these and their like are assured evidence that the Indus Civilization was mature by the time of the Sargon dynasty.

Ill. 82

But that is not all. Borings carried out in 1965 by G. F. Dales below the present level of the flood-plain at Mohenjo-daro, by the base of the so-called HR mound, produced an astonishing result. They showed that the earliest occupation begins no less than 39 ft below the present surface. If to that depth be added the height of the adjacent mound – some 30 ft – a total accumulation of nearly 70 ft must be accepted. And since no excavator has yet penetrated downwards through the 25 ft of water which drown the lower strata, the Mesopotamian contacts of about 2300 BC must have come from relatively high levels. At the same time it remains to be proved that

Ills. 83, 84

82 Borings at Mohenjo-daro in 1965 have revealed that evidence of occupation extends to a depth of 39 ft below the present flood-plain. This is an amazing fact when it is considered that the adjacent mound rises some 30 ft above the flood-plain, therefore indicating a total depth of occupation debris approaching 70 ft

the lowest levels are of the Harappan culture, and not rather of some preceding variant.

Be it repeated that in 1946, on the new Mesopotamian dating, I suggested the period 2500–1500 BC as a maximum bracket for the Indus Civilization, without any emphasis on the terminal figures. Recently, on the basis of the new radio-carbon dates, mostly from the important but relatively minor sites of Lothal and Kalibangan, it has been proposed to reduce the bracket to something like 2300–1750 BC. These contracted dates may be approximately correct for the two sites named, but the still newer evidence of the borings at Mohenjo-daro makes it difficult to apply them to the great capital city. Admittedly, too little is at present known about the nature of the immense accumulation at Mohenjo-daro; meanwhile, the whole problem of the initial date of the Civilization must remain open. What of its ending?

The End of the Indus Civilization

For a Civilization so widely distributed, no uniform ending need be postulated. Circumstances which affected it in the sub-montane lands of the central Indus may well have differed widely from those which it encountered south or east of the Indian Desert and in the watery coastlands of the Rann of Kutch. And the evidence at present available indicates that such was indeed the case.

But before embarking upon details it is well to consider for a moment the general nature of the problem. Let it be said at once that the factors instrumental in the decline and fall of historic civilizations have rarely or never been of a single uncomplicated kind. Writers, sometimes with a political or even a scientific bias, have tended to simplify beyond the likelihood of truth. Relatively modern schools of writers have tried to impose the disasters of fatal wars upon capitalism, or even upon capitalists of a particular race. A historian of high repute prefers to regard war

83, 84 The lowest levels of Mohenjo-daro have never been reached by excavation due to difficulties of a high water-table. The two photographs illustrate an attempt made with pumps in 1950 to reach the lower levels and the subsequent flooding which happened overnight

per se, without qualification, as the source of national or cultural downfall. Other theorists have blamed climate, or the malarial mosquito, as over-all causes. Others again prefer to stigmatize racial degeneration, variously defined or generously vague. Recently, violent geomorphological changes have been blamed for the end of the Indus Civilization. In a particular context which other writers have either enlarged or decried beyond warrant, I once light-heartedly blamed Indra and his Aryans for this phenomenon. The list need not be extended. In any particular instance, any one of these or other causes is likely to be fallacious in isolation. The fall, like the rise, of a civilization is a highly complex operation which can only be distorted and falsified by easy simplification. It may be taken as axiomatic that there is no one cause of cultural collapse.

To return now to the Indus Civilization, enquiry has quite naturally tended to centre upon the great city, Mohenjo-daro itself. Although its lower levels, now known to be extensive in depth, remain unexplored, enough has been brought to light – if in sketchy fashion – to suggest certain special lines of enquiry. Notable is the recurrence of deep layers of riverine or even marine deposit on at least three (probably more) occasions. The word 'marine' is here inserted tentatively on the strength of the recently recorded occurrence of marine or partially salt-water mollusca at Amri (see above) in the pre-Harappan or non-Harappan layers and recurring thence in varying but generally diminishing quantities throughout the Harappan occupation of the site, though here without any hint of deep water-laid deposit. Whether modern methods will reveal similar evidence at Mohenjo-daro, 100 miles farther inland, remains to be seen.

Anticipating this new evidence, it has recently been pointed out by R. L. Raikes, as an experienced hydrologist who has worked much in the Indus region, that significant signs are accumulating of marked coastal uplifts along the northern flank of the Arabian Sea, not earlier than Harappan times. In particular, important exploration carried out in 1960 by G. F. Dales along the shores of Makran identified derelict beaches inland from the present shore, and, what is more important, demonstrated that the Harappan sites of Sutkagen Dor (re-surveyed by Dales), and Sotka Koh (found by him near Pasni), to which must be added Bala Kot (discovered by Raikes near Sonmiani, 45 miles north-west of Karachi), make sense only as coastal stations operating in connection with a regular maritime trade. Today Sutkagen Dor is 35 miles, Sotka Koh 8 miles, and Bala Kot 12 miles from the sea. As Dales observes, 'Three natural forces have worked together . . .; the still continuing uplift of the coast, the rapid alluvial build-up at the mouths of the Dasht and

Shadi Kaur rivers (respectively associated with the two sites) and the steady building of beaches through the deposition of sand by wave action.' He adds, 'It would take only a relatively slight depression of the coastal strip and the disappearance of three to four thousand years of alluvial deposit to allow the Arabian Sea to reach the 35 miles north that Sutkagen Dor now lies from the sea.' And similarly at Sotka Koh.

It is unlikely, Raikes points out, that this coastal uplift, which appears to have affected 300 miles of the Makran coast, was limited to that area. Whether it was in any way connected with the undoubted floods which left deep deposits in southern Mesopotamia in and about the third millennium has not yet been adequately considered. It is easier to suppose that the process may have extended, in fluctuations, to the neighbouring Indus Valley in Lower Sind, where it would result in a periodical ponding back of estuarine and flood waters, and might reasonably explain the intermittent and abnormal swamping which seems to have occurred both at Mohenjo-daro and at Chanhu-daro. No alternative explanation readily presents itself. When the results of the recent borings at Mohenjo-daro have been analysed, it may be found that the great depth of occupation which they show is inflated by yet further deep-water deposits arising from this cause, and indicating that the over-all depth is not itself a fair index of the active duration of the city. But much more work will have to be done before this repetitive inflation is much more than a scientific guess.

From whatever cause, the intermittent floods at Mohenjo-daro (and at Chanhu-daro) no doubt helped, by a process of attrition, to wear down the morale of the inhabitants, and may well have contributed to the progressive deterioration which has long been recognized in their civic standards. For one thing is clear about the end of Mohenjo-daro: the city was already slowly dying before

85 As houses fell into decay so new ones of shoddier quality were built on top of their remains. The photograph shows the top of the granary at Mohenjo-daro and the new walls, built high up, can be seen clearly on the column of debris left by the excavations to support them to the right of the central figure

Ills. 85–87 ·

its ultimate end. Houses, mounting gradually upon the ruins of their predecessors or on artificial platforms in the endeavour to out-top the floods, were increasingly shoddier in construction, increasingly carved up into warrens for a swarming lower-grade population. To a height of 30 ft or more, the tall podium of the Great Granary on the western fringe of the citadel was engulfed by rising structures of poorer and poorer quality. Economic decline is everywhere apparent, and, apart altogether from the genetic decay of racial character which is an uneasy postulate, practical and immediate reasons may be inferred. The untiring consumption of major vegetation implied by the firing, age after age, of millions of bricks may, even with the aid of hill-timbers, have helped to bare the land and, by reducing the transpiration of moisture, have impaired

86 Once the neat gridiron pattern of streets and lanes of Mohenjo-daro (*cf. Ill. 14*) began to be broken up all civic pride seems to have been lost. The later (higher) buildings are in most instances merely hovels which huddle together in a rabbit-warren of buildings to house a swarming lower-grade population

the climate without drastically altering it. Over-grazing may have been an additional cause. The abnormal and smothering floods already discussed must have destroyed normal processes of irrigation; even in a brief phase of neglect, the land, with its heavy salt-content, readily turns sour. I have suggested that Mohenjo-daro was steadily wearing out its landscape; alternatively, Mohenjo-daro was being steadily worn out by its landscape. And trade, particularly with the markets of Mesopotamia, seems in the second millennium – for reasons unknown – to have become more indirect and complicated, and, no doubt, proportionately less profitable than in earlier days of more direct shipment. In one way and another, Mohenjo-daro was declining to a fall. And its later phases are sufficiently emphatic to suggest that lesser sites on the Indus axis must, from an economic point of view at least, have shared a comparable fate.

What brought the final blow, the *coup de grâce*, to the dying Civilization? Years ago, I suggested the Aryan invaders of the north-west of the subcontinent as ultimate agents of destruction. This cannot be proved and may be quite incorrect, but it is not an impossibility. There is at least no evidence that the floods which are now a popular hypothesis marked the conclusive phase. There is no sign of a final cataclysmic submergence of the topless towers, either of Mohenjo-daro or of Harappā. On the other hand, the possibility has often been remarked that in the modern place-name Harappā may be recognized the Hari-Yūpūyā which is mentioned in the Rig Veda – the early hymnal that reflects the Aryan invasions – as the scene of a defeat of the non-Aryan inhabitants by the invaders.

And in a more general sense, the picture presented by the Rig Veda is consistent with the sort of situation which may have accompanied the end of the Civilization in the Indus Valley itself. In the Vedic hymns, the Aryan invasion of the Land of the Five (originally Seven) Rivers, the Punjab and its environs, constantly assumes the form of an onslaught upon the walled cities of the aborigines. For these cities the term *pur* ('rampart', 'fort' or 'stronghold') is used. The citadel may be of stone (*aśmamayī*); alternatively, the use of mud bricks is perhaps alluded to by the epithet *āmā* ('raw', 'unbaked'). Indra, the Aryan war-god, is *puramdara*, 'fort-destroyer'. He shatters 'ninety forts' for his Aryan protégé, Divodasa. In brief, he 'rends forts as age consumes a garment'.

Where are – or were – these citadels? The discovery of fortified mounds at Harappā and Mohenjo-daro, at the Harappan sites of Sutkagen Dor in Makran, Ali Murad in Sind, and now at Kalibangan in Rajasthan has suggested that these may represent the strongholds of Indra's enemies. At any rate, up to the present no rivals to them

87 When later buildings were built on top of the remains of the earlier Mohenjo-daro foundations, wells, etc., were sunk down into the lower levels. This can give rise to the curious situation illustrated. The well, for that is what the tall 'chimney' actually is, belongs to a later building. Its lip projected only just clear of the courtyard in which it was dug (*cf. Ill. 19*), but excavation down its shaft has revealed the earlier buildings through which it was sunk, leaving it free-standing

have been identified. Unhappily the date or dates of the Aryan invasions of north-western India are largely a matter of guesswork. It is sufficiently safe to suppose that they occurred somewhere in the second millennium BC; perhaps towards the middle of the millennium, though that measure of precision exceeds the evidence.

At this point reference may be made yet again to the half-dozen groups of skeletons which are recorded from upper layers of Mohenjo-daro. Successive writers, including perhaps myself, have given them an unnecessary notoriety, but that is not to say that they are insignificant. Unfortunately, most of them are very inadequately recorded. It has been disputed both that they are all of the same period, and that that period was the latest phase of the city; though all seem to have lain at a high stratigraphic level. Certainly some of them belong to the town's

Ills. 88–91

88, 89 Many instances of sudden and violent death were found by the excavations in the uppermost levels of Mohenjo-daro. This is well illustrated in the vertical photograph, left, of skeletons sprawled in a room in 'HR Area'. The high stratigraphical position of these remains is shown in the oblique photograph, right, of these same skeletons. Many of the original reports of the excavation of groups of these massacre victims are confused in detail, hence *Ill. 89* is important evidence in showing the skeletons in relation to the latest levels of the site

Ill. 90

Ills. 88, 89

last moments. Two skeletons in 'DK Area' lay across the steps leading down to a well at the latest level, and two others in the street outside. In 'VS Area', in a street between Houses XVIII and XXXIII, a group of six skeletons, including a child, lay sprawled in a lane between houses which, whatever the date of their construction, were still standing in the last phase. It was vaguely stated that 'from their position they appear to be posterior to the adjacent remains'. In a room of 'HR Area' fourteen skeletons of men, women and a child, some of them wearing ornaments of the Indus period, were found in attitudes suggesting simultaneous and violent death; two of the skulls showed cuts by axe or sword. Their stratigraphical position is uncertain. The report is indeed almost unbelievably confused; 'it is quite likely that the skeletons belong to the interval between Intermediate I and Late III Periods, though the possibility of their being posterior to the Late Period I may be admitted'. Potentiality could

scarcely be wider; but in so far as pictorial evidence is valid, the photograph, here reproduced, shows the group on what would appear to have been the highest level. Less doubt attaches to a group of five skeletons, including (it is understood) a woman and child, found in 1964–65 in 'HR Area' by G.F. Dales amidst broken brick and debris in a lane flanked by the high walls of the latest houses. It would appear that this last group had been caught sheltering behind a dog-leg corner in the lane. Yet another group of nine skeletons in 'DK Area', amongst them five children, all 'in strangely contorted attitudes and crowded together' differs, it seems, in that the bodies may have been 'thrown pell-mell into a hurriedly made pit'; but the excavator (Mackay) goes on with the baffling observation that 'for convenience' sake the burial-place is termed a pit, but it had no defined walls nor even showed traces of having been dug!' Once more, where are we? There were two elephant tusks with the party, and Mackay suggests

Ill. 89

Ill. 91

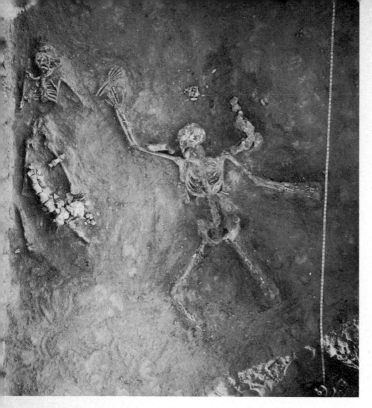

90, 91 The two skeletons, left, were found in 'DK Area' at Mohenjo-daro in a street where they fell. The photograph opposite shows a group of five skeletons, recently (1964) excavated in 'HR Area' by Dr George F. Dales. They were found in the corner of a dog-leg lane, where they had presumably been sheltering from the invaders. The brick walls and the debris in the lane belong to the latest phase of occupation

that the skeletons were remains of a family, some of them ivory-workers, 'who tried to escape with their belongings at the time of the raid but were stopped and slaughtered by the raiders'. The corpses had then been hastily covered as so much debris, without funeral-rites. As to period, one skeleton was wearing a bracelet of Indus type; the bones lay over a mass of broken masonry of 'Intermediate III Phase' and were therefore later than that; and the excavator's conclusion, for what it is worth, was that 'it was quite possible that the tragedy took place in the Late Ia Phase'.

The surprising and significant thing about this last group is that it is the only one which is thought to have been deliberately covered, however summarily, shortly after death. Particularly in the East, where decay is rapid, bodies are not left lying about amongst inhabited houses. The general inference from the thirty or more derelict

corpses at Mohenjo-daro is that from the moment of
death the place was uninhabited. The absence of skeletons
(so far) from the citadel may imply that the raiders
occupied and cleared this commanding position for their
own momentary use. For the rest, it may be suspected
that sporadic fires in the sacked city kept predatory
animals away.

Having said all this, I will merely add the comment
that the end of Mohenjo-daro, if it was marked by a
massacre as the evidence at present quite unquestionably
indicates, was rooted in deeper causes of decline; which
may well have included disastrous floods, salination of
the soil, obstructed irrigation, and even an element of the
truth embodied in Samuel Butler's plaint that 'Life is one
long process of getting tired'. Certainly the ultimate factor
is, in some measure at least, the human factor, which is in
the last issue incalculable.

CHAPTER THREE

After the Indus Civilization

In the North-west

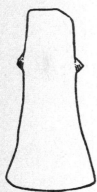

What was the sequel? The present evidence, unimpressive in bulk, suggests that the Indus 'empire' (if its wide expanse may justify that nickname) was followed by a long phase of cultural fragmentation, not altogether unlike that from which it sprang but including, perhaps, remoter exotic elements At Harappā the Indus city was succeeded, perhaps after an appreciable interval by a culture identified as 'Cemetery H' from the name of a burial-ground which overlay the true Harappan remains. The Cemetery H people produced sketchy, ill-conditioned buildings and good painted pottery which includes a few semi-Harappan elements but is essentially distinct. The culture seems to be confined to a patch of the middle Indus but has been inadequately explored. Eighty miles south of Mohenjo-daro, the little Indus town of Chanhu-daro was succeeded by two successive squatter-cultures of low grade, known respectively by the place-names 'Jhukar' and 'Jhangar', and the same thing happened to Amrī, 30 miles away. The Jhukar villagers made coarse pottery and used round button-seals, commonly bearing radiate or compartmental patterns reminiscent of second-millennium types in northern Iran and the Caucasus. Again, at Moghul Ghundai in the Zhob valley of northern

· A copper trunnion-axe (front and side view) from the Kurram valley

93 A burial in a pot (here sawn in two) from cemetery H at Harappā. The people buried here are of a later culture than the true Harappan remains which were overlaid by the cemetery

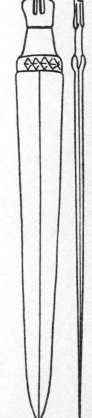

Baluchistan, burial-cairns have produced a tripod-jar, horse-bells, rings and bangles which have been compared with equipment of about 1000 BC from 'Cemetery B' at Siyalk in central Iran, but may be later. Stray finds, such as the famous bronze dagger of about the twelfth century BC from Fort Munro in the Sulaiman Range west of the Indus, and a copper trunnion axe from the Kurram valley on the Afghan border, point similarly westwards to Iran and the Caucasus. The general sense of this very scrappy material is, as a whole, that of local·poverty-stricken cultures deriving a little from a sub-Indus heritage but also drawing elements from the north-west – from the direction, in fact, of the Aryan invasions. Materially there is a notable absence of any real continuity in the Indus valley between the great Civilization and its beggarly successors.

In Saurashtra

Down the coast, on the other hand, the picture is a different one. For the moment we must rest content with a preliminary note, but it is already clear enough that in Kāthiāwād or Saurashtra – at Lothal, Rangpur, Rojdi (south of Rajkot), Somnath and other sites – and again farther south in the districts of Broach and Surat – at Mehgam and Telod on the Narbadā estuary, and at

94 A bronze dagger from Fort Munro in the Sulaiman Range west of the Indus

95 Drainage arrangements at Lothal, as on other Indus Civilization sites, were very well organized. This typical street shows a main drain in the centre with the individual drains leading down to it from the houses on the left

Bhagatrav on that of the Kim – the Indus culture shades off into sub-Indus and 'successor' cultures without dramatic break. This evidence is new and important.

Here a word of caution is appropriate. The process which I have just called 'shading off' from the recognized Indus culture to those which (in time or place) are peripheral to it requires watchful definition by archaeologists if confusion is to be avoided. In particular, it is necessary to review quite clearly the minimum qualifications required of a culture before the specific term 'Indus' can be applied to it. I would suggest the following as alternative or accumulative requirements: (i) Indus seals; (ii) Indus script, whether on seals or on pottery; (iii) certain distinctive decorative motifs on pottery, e.g. intersecting circles, scale-pattern (though this occurs at pre-Harappan Kot Diji), pipal-leaves, rosettes and peacocks in the Indus manner; (iv) certain distinctive ceramic forms, e.g. goblets with pointed base, cylindrical vessels with perforations

Ill. 43

Ills. 74, 75

Ill. 76

96 Lothal shows all the normal characteristics of an Indus Civilization site in its straight streets, drains (*Ill. 95*, opposite), granary and platform. In all there were six phases of occupation and the orderly arrangement of houses and streets is well illustrated in this view over the site. See *Ill. 38* for the dock at Lothal

(colanders), tall jars with S-shaped profile and ledged rims, and 'fruit-dishes' or 'dishes-on-stand', though these last *may* occur outside the Indus culture proper; (v) triangular terracotta 'cakes'; (vi) kidney-shaped inlays of shell or faïence; (vii) certain beads, notably discoidal with tubular piercing.

Ill. 74

Ill. 24
Ill. 72

No doubt in time other forms or categories will be found to mark provincial or late varieties of the Indus Civilization; meanwhile, caution may again be urged in the use of the term 'Indus'.

With this proviso, it is now becoming possible in Saurashtra (Kāthiāwāḍ) and even farther south, to identify a late and developing branch of the Indus Civilization, varying perhaps locally and extending downwards in time towards 1600 BC. For this branch I propose the specific name 'Saurashtrian Indus'.

Up to date, Lothal, with its straight streets, drains, granary and platform, and with six phases of occupation,

Ills. 95, 96

is the best-known of these Saurashtrian sites, it has been
well excavated by S. R. Rao. Numerous steatite seals and
some of the pottery make it impeccably 'Indus'. At the
same time, its ceramic decoration tails off into friezes of
birds, caprids (the goat family) and trees, with less
affinity to Indus fashions than to some of those of the
Central Indian chalcolithic (Malwa and the Narbadā
region). New types also, such as a stud-handled vessel
which is likely to become a 'type-fossil', occur here but
not on the Indus. Above all, a constant though subordinate accompaniment of these Indus and sub-Indus
fabrics is a Black-and-Red Ware, variegated by inverted
firing – a procedure widely diffused in time and place both
in and outside India – and sometimes roughly decorated
with white lines and dots. There is less and less doubt
that here we have the germ of the Black-and-Red pottery
which was to be the constant accompaniment of the
megalithic culture of central and southern India in the
latter half of the first millennium B C.

Lothal is not alone in this evidence. At Rojdi, farther
north near Rajkot, is another sub-Indus site, the authen-
ticity of which is established by an Indus-script graffito;
and here too the Black-and-Red fabric occurs alongside
the sub-Indus wares. So, too, at Rangpur, 30 miles from
Lothal, the Black-and-Red occurred with a 'late' Indus
culture which itself culminated in a 'Lustrous Red Ware'
alien to the Indus Valley. In one way and another the
Saurashtrian Indus Civilization is a provincial variant of
the metropolitan culture, with a measurable element of
local enterprise and a leaning towards the Centre and the
South.

The circumstances in which these and other Harappan
sites came into being as far south as the Gulf of Cambay
are naturally conjectural. There is accumulative evidence
that they began only after the Indus Civilization was
firmly established in its name-home. It may be that the

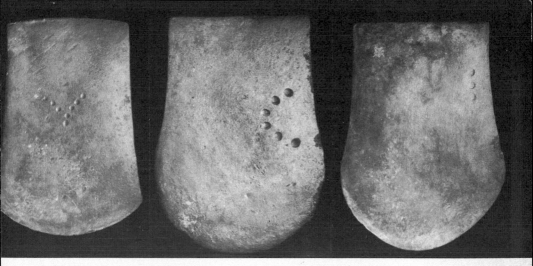

expansion along the coastlands was a positive sequel to developing maritime trade towards the Persian Gulf. On the other hand if the (now fashionable) uplift-theory, whereby a rising shore-line in the neighbourhood of the Indus estuary ponded back the Lower Indus and partially drowned its valley, turns out to be a correct diagnosis, it may be feasible to suspect a negative refugee-element in this southerly colonization. Or again, the explanation may be a combination of the two, on the sound principle that simple explanations are generally wrong. Certainty is not in sight.

In Central India

Two scraps of evidence with a possible bearing upon an inter-regional linkage between the Saurashtrian 'Indus' and Central India may be mentioned. The microlithic blade industries which characterized central India in and before the earlier half of the first millennium B C sometimes include parallel-sided blades of a more formidable type, comparable with the chert blades of the Indus valley and Baluchistan. At Maski in Andhra Pradesh, for example, they run to more than 5 ins in length. Apart altogether from the fortuitous availability of material, it is difficult not to suppose that we have here a genuine intrusion from the north-west, no doubt through Saurashtra. And again the flat copper axes which occur on chalcolithic sites at Jorwe (a hoard of six),

east of Bombay, and at Navdatoli on the central Narbadā are of an Indus type; and though they are of an
unspecialized kind, they are consistent with a measure of
cultural intercommunication between the lower Indus and
the Narbadā system by way of the west coast. The
evidence adds up.

A possible further link between central and Harappan
India at this period may deserve consideration when more
evidence is available. At present our knowledge of the
earlier history of rice is disproportionately meagre in
view of its wide importance in medieval and modern
times. It would indeed be difficult to over-emphasize the
participation of this grain in the physical and even the
mental make-up of those many millions who have made
it the main basis of their diet. Combined of course with
many other factors, it has helped to condition a way of
life which is – or was until recently – distinctive of regions
and peoples. The wheat-eating peasant of the Punjab and
the rice-eating peasant of Bengal are recognizably sun-
dered from one another in spite of sporadic bonds of
religion and a general community of standards. There is
room for a fresh study of the influences of diet, coupled
with variant agricultural routines, upon mind and habit.

Now rice-impressions have been recognized at the
Harappan site of Lothal in Phase A, which on radio-
carbon dating lasted until 1700 BC or somewhat later. At
about the same time, rice appears in periods II–IV on the
little site of Navdatoli, far away on the central reaches of
the Narbadā or Narmadā. Here radio-carbon analysis
gives a date of 1660 BC ± 130 for a late level of Period II.
In Period I, which seems not to have been very much
earlier, wheat had been used, but not rice; so that, if the
evidence is representative, rice was known in western
India in the eighteenth century BC, and in central India
perhaps a century later. No earlier dates for the grain
appear at present to be available anywhere.

98, 99   The pottery from the site of Navdatoli is very distinctive. It includes graceful stemmed cups ('champagne' or 'brandy glasses') and bowls of a pale yellowish ware with black geometrical patterns which are finely executed

Navdatoli (beginning about the seventeenth century BC) has been mentioned and, by virtue of its extensive excavation by Professor H. D. Sankalia, further particulars may be added. The site lies opposite Maheshwar, at the southern end of an ancient crossing of the Narbadā, and derives its present name (and no doubt its traditonal avocation) from the *navdas* or boatmen who constitute most of the male population of the adjacent modern village. The ancient site occupies four small mounds within an area little more than 400 yds square on the topmost terrace of the valley.

From the outset the huts of this chalcolithic village were built of timber posts and bamboo screens, on square or oblong plans; circular structures were probably store-rooms. The floors were of clay and cow-dung with a thin coating of lime and must originally, as the excavator remarks, have looked tolerably spick and span. Equipment included 'copper' flat-axes, fish-hooks, pins and rings, with an abundant blade-industry of stone, the blades ranging from 1 to 2 ins and showing occasional retouch. As a whole, this stone industry (generally of agate or chalcedony) may be described as microlithic of

Ill. 97

91

100 Painted pottery sherds from Navdatoli showing dancing stylized human figures

Ills. 98, 99

Ill. 100

an unevolved kind. The pottery on the other hand showed an unusual distinction. Apart from store-jars it included graceful cups on stems ('champagne' or 'brandy glasses') of pale yellowish ware with black geometrical patterns; and vases of similar ware with outlined animal-patterns or rows of highly stylized human figures, dancing. There are also bowls with more or less horizontal open-topped spouts, in origin a metallic type which has been speculatively derived from Iran; but the Iranian 'prototypes' were, on the present dating, several centuries later, and in any case there are no known intermediary links in the 1200 miles of intervening Asia.

In Malwa and other regions of central India, sites of this general kind, chalcolithic with a simplified microlithic industry and with pottery inclined to local fashion, are gradually being brought to light. They are variously ascribed to the second and early first millennium BC, but require more radio-carbon dating for certainty. Though full of regional and even aggregate interest, they never rise to the status of 'civilization'; they were essentially village cultures. Civilization in those parts had to wait until fresh elements arrived in or about the fifth century BC from a new direction, furnished with a new metal. That will be Section 3 of the story of civilization in India; for Section 2 we must turn to the Ganges basin, with a side-glance to partially concurrent happenings in the north-west frontier.

CHAPTER FOUR

The Ganges Basin

Vagabond Craftsmen

The exploration of the two-river country, or *doāb*, of the Ganges-Jumna (Gangā-Yamunā) basin is still in a rudimentary stage. Within the *doāb*, the first archaeological event (in terms of post-palaeolithic time) which calls for notice is the occurrence over a wide stretch of country of a distinctive series of hoards of copper, rarely bronze, objects which are readily recognizable though still inadequately understood. They comprise eight main types: (i) flat axes, usually of stocky sub-rectangular form with splayed edge; (ii) shouldered axes with a clear kink or set-back at the points where the curved edge meets the stem of the implement; (iii) bar-celts or chisels, up to 2 ft long, consisting of a nearly parallel-sided bar and an expanded chisel-edge in one of the lateral planes, not central as in the axes; (iv) rings made by bending a rod of circular section until the ends meet; (v) harpoon-heads strangely like the Magdalenian or Azilian horn harpoons of the West, with bilateral barbs and a loop or projection for the attachment of a cord; (vi) spearheads (sometimes called swords) with strong mid-rib and often with a projection from the tang for the attachment of a cord; (vii) swords, usually with the hilt or tang of one piece with the blade and bifurcated like antennae; and (viii) strange

Ill. 101

Ill. 102

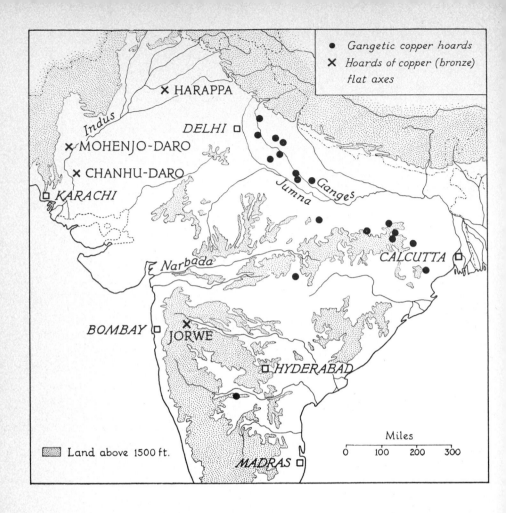

anthropomorphic objects, up to 18 ins long, which might
be taken to represent a human form with straddled legs
and incurved arms. Their purpose and whether indeed
their anthropomorphism is intentional are alike unknown.

Some thirty-four sites have produced implements of
these types, mostly in hoards from Uttar Pradesh, Madhya
Pradesh, Vindhya Pradesh, Bihar, Andhra Pradesh, West
Bengal and Orissa. The only specimen found in a significant context is the fragment of an anthropomorph from
the Harappan site of Lothal in Saurashtra; but, useful
though this solitary stray be as an indication that the type
existed, at least as scrap, not much later than the eighteenth

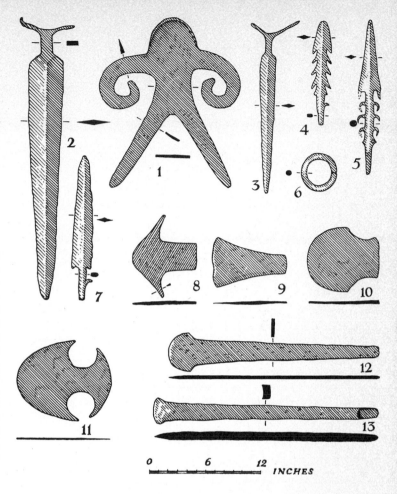

101 The distribution of Gangetic copper hoards and hoards of copper flat-axes

102 Examples of finds from Gangetic copper hoards: 1, 'anthropomorph' from Sheorājpur; 2, 3, antennae swords from Fategarh; 4, 5, harpoons from Sarthaulī and Bisaulī; 6, ring from Pandi; 7, 8, hooked spear and axe from Sarthaulī; 9, axe from Gungariā; 10, axe from Dunriā; 11, double axe from Shagrā Pīr; 12, 13, bar-celts from Gungariā

0   6   12   INCHES

or seventeenth century B C, it is culturally out of context in a Harappan environment. For the rest, no hint is available as to the dating of these hoards, unless it be their complete absence from the numerous sites which have produced the now familiar Painted Grey Ware. This ware (see below, p. 98) marks the earliest mature civilization of the Gangetic plain and is ascribable to the first half of the first millennium B C. The non-association may safely be taken to imply that the hoards are earlier than *c.* 1000 B C; a bracket of *c.* 1700–1000 B C is probably therefore wide enough to catch them, wide enough too to emphasize the need for much more precise knowledge.

Ills. 104, 106

What do the hoards themselves tell us? The flat axes with more or less expanded blades are the only formal link with the Indus Civilization, and the type is too generalized and widespread to support the view, which has been stated, that the hoards represent 'the colonization of the Ganges basin by refugees and displaced persons from the Punjab and the Indus Valley during the time of the break-up of the Harappā Empire and the coming of raiders from the west'. An alternative theory that the hoards may be 'in fact traces of the Indo-Aryan migration' is equally difficult to sustain. They cannot be traced to any source outside India; and in any event the term 'Indo-Aryan' relates to language, not to material culture.

Nevertheless, these remarkable hoards are not completely dumb. The axes, up to a foot in length and five or six pounds in weight, are excellent woodmen's tools. The barbed harpoons, based perhaps on horn or bone prototypes, proclaim extensive food-gathering in the fishful rivers near which they are found. That they were also used for hunting animals as formidable as the rhinoceros is shown by cave-paintings of unknown date in the Mirzapur district of the Ganges valley, south-west of Banaras. Only the swords which occur on four of the sites imply a more military element, in view of their scarcity symbolical perhaps of rank rather than recurrent peril. The general inference is that the hoards represent semi-nomadic food-gathering communities, capable of clearing patches of jungle and perhaps (though this we do not know) of some sort of garden-agriculture, but living mainly by hunting and fishing. The likelihood fits in well with far more modern pictures of tribal India. It has, however, been further inferred that the deposition of the hoards indicates a time of insecurity and economic instability, such as may be postulated in the period of the (supposed) secondary Aryan invasion of the northern plains. Once more the omnipresent Aryans are allowed to force the material

Ill. 102

evidence beyond its warrant. All that can be safely said is that the copper implements are shown, by their frequently specialized character and skilful casting and hammering, and by their distribution over 800 miles of jungle landscape, to have been the work of substantially whole-time experts who were probably also (as in other parts of the world) itinerant. The perils of one kind and another which must have beset them in their vagrancy and led to the occasional loss of their stock-in-trade were not necessarily more formidable than those which man and beast would normally impose upon the wandering craftsman and tradesman in the rough circumstances of the age. Once more it is unnecessary or premature to conjure up cosmic causes such as Aryan invasion to explain these sporadic casualties.

Ill. 101

The Ganges Civilization

We may be content, then, to leave in suspense this preliminary episode in the post-Stone Age archaeology of the Gangetic plains. That, however, is not necessarily to shake off what may be called the Aryan pursuit. For following – at what stretch of time we know not – the anonymous copper hoards, there arose in the same region with seeming suddenness an evolved and widespread urban culture almost worthy of the name 'civilization'. Its origins, historical or archaeological, are unknown, though it clearly deserves a respectable parentage. If the hoards are not Aryan why should this new and burgeoning urbanity claim the title? The claim has indeed been made, but there is no particle of evidence for (or against) it. Let us admit uncompromisingly that no 'Aryan culture' has yet been isolated anywhere in India as a material and recognizable phenomenon, and pass on to the facts.

These are meanwhile of adequate interest in themselves. Three sites will here suffice to show the sort of evidence that is likely to be forthcoming from many more. At Hastināpura in the upper Ganges valley the succession of

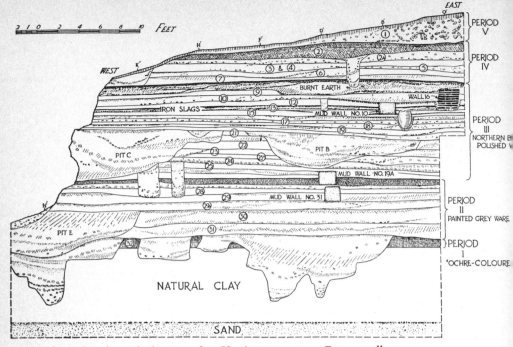

Labels visible in the figure:
WEST — EAST
FEET (scale: 2 1 0 2 4 6 8 10)
PERIOD V
PERIOD IV
PERIOD III — NORTHERN BLACK POLISHED WARE
PERIOD II — PAINTED GREY WARE
PERIOD I — 'OCHRE-COLOURED'
BURNT EARTH
IRON SLAGS
WALL 16
MUD WALL NO. 10
MUD WALL NO. 19A
MUD WALL NO. 31
PIT C
PIT B
PIT E
NATURAL CLAY
SAND

103 A section through the mound at Hastināpura, upper Ganges valley

Ill. 103

cultures has been established by careful digging, and is as follows. The earliest phase, Period I, is represented by a thin layer containing rough ochre-coloured pottery of a kind which has been noted on several sites from Bikaner eastwards. It is not, as yet, associated with buildings but may possibly be related (though this is unproved) to the copper hoards described above. Civic life in recognizable form begins only with Period II, in the earlier half of the first millennium BC, with remains of mud or mud brick walls of unascertained plan, associated with a hard and distinctive grey painted pottery with black linear patterns,

Ill. 104

already described as the Painted Grey Ware. No microliths or other stone implements are associated with this ware, but copper (very rarely iron, but see below, p. 113, in connection with Atranjikhera) was used for arrowheads and other tools and weapons. The humped bull, buffalo, sheep and pig were domesticated, and cultivated grains included the now familiar rice. The date of this urban culture, with its mixed farming, seems to have been

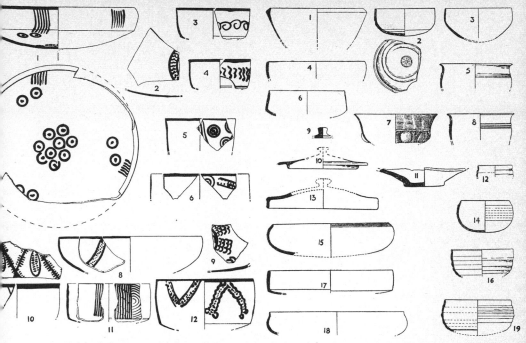

104, 105   Painted Grey Ware, left, and Northern Black Polished Ware, right. Scale ⅙

about 1000 or 800 to 500 B C. Its earlier roots have not yet
been recognized, but the excellence of some of the Painted
Grey Ware implies an established tradition. The ware may
possibly be related, through links which have not yet
been discovered, to bowls found in secondary burials at
Shāhi Tump in Baluchistan; but this is at present mere
guesswork.

Period III at Hastināpura is marked by the full use of
iron (see below, p. 112). To the same period may be traced
the introduction of money which in India was struck at
first on the Persian standard. And shortly after the arrival
of iron a hard and distinctive glossy black ware, known as
Northern Black Polished Ware, emerged in the *doāb*, perhaps in its steel-like quality imitating polished iron.
With the emergence of the Northern Black Polished Ware,
the Painted Grey Ware went shortly out of use. Baked
bricks, as well as mud-bricks, were now used in the
buildings, and soak-pits of superimposed jars with perforated bases or of superimposed terracotta rings now

Ill. 105

Ill. 107

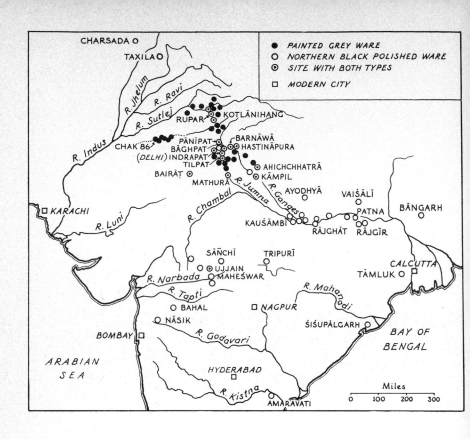

began their long life in the civic equipment of the subcontinent. The date of this phase must have approximated to 500–200 or 150 BC; the next phase, Period IV, which lacked the Northern Black Polished Ware, produced coins of Mathurā rulers ascribed to the second century BC.

On this evidence, urban life began in the *doāb* about 1000 BC, and, since that time, has been continuous there. Changes in material and craftsmanship have been subordinate to a general continuity of civic consciousness and well-being. Fertile riverside clearings in the broad jungles which then covered the great plains contained the towns and cities that are the background of the Indian epics: cities such as Hastināpura itself, which was the epic capital of the Kaurava kings, or Ahichchhatrā, near Ramnagar in Uttar Pradesh, which, as capital of North Panchālā, is likewise mentioned in the *Mahābhārata*.

106 The distribution of Painted Grey Ware and Northern Black Polished Ware

107 Soak-pits began to appear in Indian towns after 500 BC. The two examples shown are from Hastināpura and are respectively made up of superimposed jars with perforated bases and superimposed terracotta rings

The ramparts of Ahichchhatrā still rise to a majestic height above the plain and are 3½ miles in circuit. Somewhat summary excavation there has produced evidence comparable with that from Hastināpura; this is now (1965) being checked by further cuttings. The earthen ramparts are basically of two successive periods crowned by a baked-brick wall, and Painted Grey Ware is said to have been found in and below the earlier rampart, which should therefore not be much later than 500 BC and may be appreciably earlier. As at Hastināpura, coinage came into use during the succeeding Northern Black Polished Ware period, *i.e.* between the fifth and second centuries BC. The town was rebuilt on eight or nine occasions, and lasted until it was superseded by Badaun about AD 1100. A fresh exploration of the site on a considerable scale would be rewarding.

Ill. 108

A no less imposing site, indeed one of the great sites of India, is that of Kaushāmbī, beside the Jumna 30 miles from Allahābād. The earliest defences, some 4 miles in circuit and standing to a height of over 40 ft shortly preceded the introduction of Northern Black Polished Ware and may therefore be somewhat earlier than 500 B C. They consist of a mud bank revetted externally with a battered wall of baked brick which, beside the eastern gate, still remains to a height of 154 courses. Near the base this wall had begun to bulge dangerously, and rough weep-holes had been cut through it to relieve the pressure. It was subsequently renewed or replaced on more than one occasion, but the whole story of this very remarkable structure has not yet been worked out. Within the defences were well-built brick houses and a famous Buddhist Monastery, the Ghoshitārāma, of which the earliest phase has been ascribed to the century of the Buddha's death (fifth century B C) but may be somewhat later.

Other sites fit approximately into the same time-table. Vaisālī, in the Muzaffarpur district of Bihar, was the capital of the Lichchhavis, the tribe or principality which produced the Buddha, and recent excavation claims to have revealed the stupa built in the fifth century to enshrine a share of the relics of the Buddha immediately after his death. The city itself must go back to the sixth century B C or earlier. Again at Banaras or Vārānasi renewed excavations at Rajghat have shown once more that the city goes back at least to c. 500 B C, and no doubt some part of it is yet earlier. Extended exploration is here prevented by the fact that the present city, with its teeming population, spreads over the site of its predecessors and owes much of its height to their underlying accumulation.

In summary, year by year fresh evidence points to a great burgeoning of civic life on the northern plains by the second quarter of the first millennium B C.

CHAPTER FIVE

The North-west Frontier

Persians and Greeks

This has brought us to the age of the Buddha (about 500 BC) and the threshold of Indian history in the more explicit usage of the term. Before entering upon the enlarged and yet in some small measure simplified problems of this new age, it is desirable to return briefly to the north-west frontier of the subcontinent and to glance at events which had been reshaping the cultures of that stormy region and were in one way and another to have an appreciable effect upon a considerable part of the subcontinent.

There are many natural gateways into India through the mountains of the north and north-west but, save for the advent of Islam which came primarily by sea, the most important historically has always been the partial gap represented by the valley of the Kabul River or the adjacent Khyber Pass.

In the latter part of the sixth century BC the Persian Empire, probably under the leadership of Cyrus the Great (558–530 BC), was extended through the Hindu Kush into the Peshawar plain, which as Gadara or Gandhāra was catalogued by Darius I amongst his eastern satrapies or provinces in his great inscription of c. 518 BC on the rock of Behistūn in western Persia. Subsequently Darius

109, 110 The Bālā Ḥiṣār, Chārsada, rises imposingly from the
plain. In the centre of the photograph can be seen the huge excavated cut made through the defences in 1958; a closer view is
shown, right. Accumulation of
debris and buildings have raised the
height of the highest mound to 65 ft

III An aerial view of the Bālā Ḥiṣār, Chārsada, shows its present extent, about 15 acres, and also the second mound in the background representing an extension of the city subsequent to its surrender to Alexander the Great in 327 BC. At that time it was surrounded by fortifications, illustrated opposite

carried the Persian or Achaemenid suzerainty to the lands adjoining the Indus, so that 'India' (in this restricted sense) is included on his inscriptions at Persepolis and Naqsh-i-Rustam, where he was entombed in 486 BC. Herodotus a little later records 'India' as the last and richest of the satrapies.

Through these satrapies, across the middle of the Peshawar plain and the Indus above Attock, there may already have existed before these events a recognized trade-route between the subcontinent, Afghanistan and Persia. Be that as it may, an arterial highway was now established along this line under the protection of the Persian King of Kings and the stimulus of a developing imperial commerce. Towns with the status of provincial capitals grew up along it, either as new foundations or as new enlargements of established settlements. Of two of

112 Traces of the defences built against Alexander the Great's troops at Chārsada in 327 BC were identified by excavation in 1958. A ditch was found backed by an earthen rampart whose exterior had been faced with a mud-brick wall. Traces of the post-holes of a timber-lined entrance were also found

these wayside capitals something is known from excavation; at Chārsada north-east of Peshawar, and Taxila north-west of Rawalpindi.

Both sites show a wide spread of mounds with intervening gaps, indicating the removal of the town from time to time to new ground at the will of changing dynasties or fashions. (The arch-example of this oriental habit is that of Delhi, which has moved at least eight times during the past thousand years.) At Chārsada, the ancient Pushkalāvati or Peukelaōtis ('Lotus City'), former capital of Gandhāra, the highest mound, the Bālā Hiṣār or High fort, has risen by accumulation to 65 ft and represents the earliest known site of the town, originally some 15 acres in extent, in the vicinity of the junction of the rivers Kabul and Swat. This was the capital which was besieged by a division of Alexander's troops in 327

113 An intaglio impression of Athena on a clay sealing, from Chārsada, probably first century BC

107

114, 115 The aerial view of the early city of Taxila I, the Bhīr Mound, left (fifth to second centuries BC), shows none of the careful town planning characteristic look of the much earlier cities of the Indus Valley and of the later Indo-Greeks. *Ill. 115*, opposite, is a general view of Taxila II (Sirkap) showing the influence of regular Hellenistic planning, first centuries BC–AD. *Cf. Ill. 121*

Ill. 112

Ill. 127

Ill. 122

BC, and since it is recorded that it took these veterans under a trusted general thirty days to capture the place it must certainly have been fortified. In fact, a length of this fortification was identified by excavation in 1958; it consisted of a ditch backed by an earthen rampart faced externally by a wall of mud brick.

Subsequently, under the Indo-Greek rulers who, driven from Bactria, took over the frontier region and the Punjab in the second century BC, the town was moved three furlongs to the north-east and laid out on the chessboard lines which sub-Greek Bactria had no doubt inherited from the Hellenistic West. Elements of this regimented plan, on what is today known as Shaikhān Dheri, were revealed dramatically in 1958 by air-photography and have since been verified by excavation. It consists of straight main-streets 40 yds apart framing recognizable house-plans, with a temple-precinct in a somewhat wider range (50 yds) as befitted its status. Equally apparent

are the generally Western character of the lay-out and the incorporation of Eastern features within it.

Across the Indus, 125 miles from Pushkalāvati, lies the second of these caravan-cities, Taxila. Like Pushkalāvati, it was the *chef lieu* of a local principality and presumably retained a limited independence within the Persian Empire. Its earliest site, known as the Bhīr Mound, has been sufficiently excavated to show us the shambles that it was: with its conglomeration of ill-aligned and ill-built rubble which can scarcely have been disguised by former coverings of painted and unpainted plaster. Here it was that the local king with a submissive hospitality received the conquering Alexander in 326 BC; and it is a modest consolation to be told by a reputable historical tradition (via Strabo) that the local Brahman ascetics at least stood no nonsense in argument from the Western intruder.

Across a little valley, the Tamrā Nālā, however lie the expansive remains of Taxila II, commonly known as

Ills. 114, 122

Ills. 115, 121

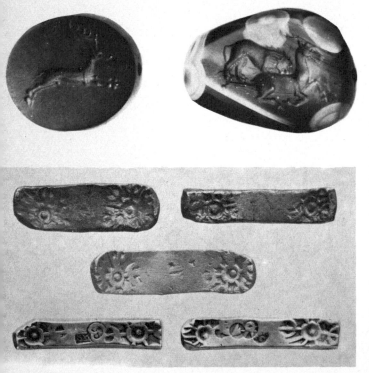

116–120 Foreign influence of Persians, Greeks and Parthians is reflected in many of the finds from Taxila (Bhīr Mound – Sirkap). *Ill. 116*, a roundel from the centre of a Graeco-Roman silver dish, shows Dionysus holding his wine cup in his right hand. *Ill. 117* is the head of a pensive youth in terracotta. Persian (Achaemenid) influence is shown in *Ills. 118, 119*, gems with lively scenes of a leaping stag and a lion attacking a stag. They were found, together with the bent-bar coins, *Ill. 120*, in the Bhīr Mound, early third century BC

121 Taxila II (Sirkap), across the valley from Taxila I, the Bhīr Mound, is completely different in its lay-out (*cf. Ill. 114*). Instead of a conglomeration of hovels this is a town laid out on a Graeco-Parthian chessboard plan in the first century AD but based probably upon the Indo-Greek city of two centuries earlier which lies beneath it.

Sirkap. Here, without particularization, it will suffice to observe the well-known vestiges of another chessboard town, superficially of Parthian origin (first century AD) but presumed to take its rectilinear plan from an Indo-Greek city (second-first century BC) which is known to exist beneath a part of it. A considerable stretch of the Parthian main street has been cleared. It has a width of 7–10 yds, runs straight southwards from the north gate and is crossed at right angles by a regular system of smaller streets at 35–45 yd intervals. A majority of the buildings lining the main street were small shops raised slightly above the street-level, as in a modern bazaar. Behind them were close-set houses, some of them planned round courtyards. Amongst other buildings accessible from the main street were a large temple and half-a-dozen small Buddhist or Jaina stupas, bearing a mixture of Graeco-Roman and Indian decoration.

Ill. 117

The sequence of Taxila (Bhīr Mound–Sirkap) thus equates with that of Pushkalāvati (Bālā Hiṣār–Shaikhan Dheri); and it is of interest to recall that in the *Ramayana*, which is after all an epic, not a history, Taxila and

Pushkalāvati are contemporary foundations by the two sons of Bharat.

The details of these successive cities need not be further considered here, but the whole complex episode – Persian and Greek – which they represent offers features of a wider interest. Alike at Chārsada's Bālā Hiṣār and at Taxila's Bhīr Mound, iron was used from the beginning as at present known. Both sites must be supposed to have existed, as caravan-cities, on the great international highway from the time of the Persian conquest, *i.e.* from *c.* 540–500 BC; the orderly functioning of this highway implies nodal centres such as they represent. In this frontier-region, therefore, iron was in use not later than the latter part of the sixth century BC.

A point of current interest here arises. The date of the first use of iron in the Indian subcontinent is at present under discussion, and new evidence which may eventually settle the matter has not yet been published. Until recently there was no good reason for supposing that the metal was in general use within the limits of the North-West Frontier until that region was absorbed, as has just been recalled, into the Persian Empire in the latter part of the sixth century BC. True, iron was familiar in Persia by the end of the second or beginning of the first millennium BC, and may have penetrated here and there into low-grade but accessible cultures on the Baluch borderlands within the first half of the first millennium. But even when it became widely known its use was liable to be patchy and restricted. As late as the earlier half of the fifth century BC the powerful Massagetae of eastern Iran are recorded to have been still without it. The earliest unequivocal literary evidences for the use of iron by Indians are the well-known references by Herodotus and Ktesias in that century. Until very recently, the earliest firm archaeological evidence for the normal use of iron within the subcontinent was provided by the first Taxila (the Bhīr

122 The regimented plan of Shaikhān Dheri half a mile from the Bālā Ḥiṣār, Chārsada, was discovered by air-photography in 1958. As it appears the plan in the aerial photograph is a 'ghost'. Its lines are not those of the true walls, they are the outlines of the robber trenches from which the baked bricks of the walls had been robbed by villagers. Excavation has since confirmed that the plan was laid out by Indo-Greeks in the second century BC

Mound), for which Sir John Marshall's initial date of about 500 BC is unlikely to be varied significantly.

Now news comes that, low down in a mound at Atranjikhera, in the Etah district of Uttar Pradesh, iron has been found by Professor Nurul Hasan and R. C. Gaur in association with Painted Grey Ware and with organic material to which a date in the vicinity of 1100 or 1000 BC has been ascribed on the results of radio-carbon analyses carried out by the Tata Institute of Fundamental Research at Bombay. All this needs careful verification, but meanwhile there is a possibility that a part of India may have marched closely with Persia in the introduction of iron-working. The early dating for Painted Grey Ware is also noteworthy. It may now appear that the earliest civilization in the Northern Plains was contemporaneous with, and no doubt stimulated by, the appearance of iron there, alongside the distinctive pottery, a little before or a little after 1000 BC.

But whether iron is or is not proved to be a Persian innovation, there can be little doubt that the use of money came to India as a Persian idea. There is no pre-Persian Indian money, and on the other hand in a variety of forms it is common enough with Northern Black Polished ware in the centuries following 500 BC. The indication is that of increasing and increasingly systematized trade, which in all probability owed a primary stimulus to the impact of Persian modes and disciplines. At the same time it may be re-emphasized that urban life in the Indian plains was amplified rather than created at this time. So far as the available evidence goes, the moneyless towns of the Painted Grey Ware period – say, 1000–500 BC – could show standards of living not vastly inferior to those of the moneyed cities which used Northern Black Polished Ware after 500 BC. True, baked bricks were now freely employed for building fortifications, houses and drains, and everywhere were efficient terracotta 'soak-wells' or 'soak-pits'; but all these would seem to represent improvement rather than revolution.

Ills. 123–125   Then in 327 BC came Alexander the Great. His intervention in central Asia was a matter of months, but its political and cultural consequences were stupendous. Its sequels were revolutions indeed. Politically it led in the north to an awakening of Indian nationalism on an unprecedented scale. Culturally it laid the foundations of much that was to become widely characteristic of Indian architecture and sculpture. It awoke the Indian genius as nothing had stirred it since the advent of the Indus Civilization or the more shadowy Aryans.

The starting-point may be traced to 330 BC, when the last Darius was murdered and his palace of Persepolis burnt about the ears of his victor. The reign of the Great Kings was over; however much Alexander might attempt, from mixed motives of humanity and interest, to protect the conquered Persian cities and to perpetuate the Achae-

123–127 It was only after Alexander the Great's death that a reasonably true likeness of him appeared on coins (*Ill. 123*). The dekadrachm, or ten-drachm piece (*Ills. 124, 125*), is an extremely rare coin struck at Babylon to commemorate Alexander's victory over King Porus in the Punjab. Alexander is shown on the obverse on horseback attacking an elephant and the reverse shows the goddess of victory, Nike, flying to crown the standing figure of Alexander. Alexander's eastern successor, Seleukos, is shown on the tetradrachm (*Ill. 126*), and the Indo-Greek King Menander, who ruled Chārsada in the second century BC, in *Ill. 127*

menid régime as its self-appointed heir, the clock could not be reversed. The Greeks passed on to claim the Persian provinces of India, and behind them two centuries of lavish royal patronage came abruptly to an end. The accumulated artistry of Persia was out of work.

The Mauryan Empire

The sequel is not difficult to reconstruct. From the Punjab Alexander withdrew westwards, to die at Babylon in 323 BC. His eastern successor, Seleukos, found himself confronted by an astonishing upsurgence of Indian nationalism led by Chandragupta, the first king of the Mauryan dynasty, from his small kingdom of Magadha by the Ganges. In the upshot, the old satrapies of 'India' and Gandhara as far as the Hindu Kush were ceded to the Indian king. He thus acquired possession of an immense new territory which, though basically non-Iranian, was prepared by long use for the circulation or transmission of Persian ideas and indeed officially employed a Persian script for its vernacular.

Here was the greatest empire that India had ever produced, greater even than that which may be accredited to

the Indus Civilization itself. Above all, here was the potential patronage of a triumphant dynasty with, as yet, no confirmed artistic tradition of its own in any way comparable with its wealth and its ambition. Here, in the new India, was a new home for the accomplished artists and craftsmen of Persia. And hither they came.

It is scarcely an exaggeration to say that the Indo-Persian phase which resulted from this convergence of need and opportunity marked the beginning of masonry architecture in India. There had of course been stone and brick buildings far back in the third millennium, though little enough to which, so far as we know, the proud term 'architecture' can be unreservedly applied. Subsequently, the earliest stone structures in India to which an approximate date can be attached are the defences of Old Rājgir in the hills of southern Bihār. These great defences, 25 miles in length, enclose the site of the city which, as the capital of the kingdom of Magadha, achieved distinction in the sixth century B C by association with the

Ill. 129

128, 129 The defences at Old Rājgir run intermittently for 25 miles. Illustrated opposite is a detail of the town wall; and the way in which the bastions stood out square from the wall can be seen in the overall view of a stretch of the wall, right

Buddha and Mahāvīra during the first formative period of the Buddhist and Jaina cults. The work consists of a massive wall, dry-built of large unshapen stones, with square bastions at frequent intervals: not much to show as evidence of architectural sensibility. But the foundations of a new order were laid when the rulers of Magadha in the fifth century BC built a fortress on the plain beside the rivers Ganges and Son where the straggling town of Patna now stands. This fortress of Paṭali was enlarged into the splendid capital city of Pāṭaliputra by the first Mauryan emperor about 320 BC.

Ill. 128

Of the new metropolis archaeologists, working in the arduous conditions of a waterlogged site, have told us enough to lend credence to the scraps of information which have come to us deviously from Megasthenes, the envoy of Seleukos at the Mauryan court about 302 BC. In his day, Pāṭaliputra formed an oblong over 9 miles long beside the river, and over a mile wide. It was fortified by a ditch 200 yds broad and a timber palisade with towers

Ill. 130

and loop-holes for archers. In the royal palace there was
much that was 'calculated to excite admiration, and with
which neither Susa, with all its costly splendour, nor
Ekbatana, with all its magnificence, can vie. In the parks
tame peacocks are kept, and pheasants which have been
domesticated; and cultivated plants . . . and shady groves
and pastures planted with trees, and tree-branches which
the art of the woodman has deftly interwoven. . . . There
are also tanks of great beauty in which they keep fish of
enormous size but quite tame'. The whole description is
significantly reminiscent of a Persian 'paradise', and there
can be no doubt as to whence the general character of
Chandragupta's palace was derived.

Though no excavation commensurate with the importance of the site has been carried out here, preliminary
attempts have not been unrewarded. Lengths of imposing
timber framework discovered in 1926–7 testify to the
general credibility of Megasthenes's account of the fortification. But of more specific importance is the masonry

130 A timber palisade with towers and a ditch 200 yards broad formed the defences at Pāṭaliputra

131 A Mauryan column-capital, third century BC, found at Pāṭaliputra in 1896, shows distinct Persian influence in its side-volutes and central palmettes

which has from time to time been brought to the surface. As long ago as 1896 a column-capital with stepped impost, side-volutes and central palmettes of Persian type was found, and the fragment of another with Achaemenian palmette and bead-and-reel pattern was unearthed in 1955. The latter, of polished sandstone, recalls the high polish which the Mauryan masons copied from the Persians. (The masonry of the palace of Darius and Xerxes at Persepolis, for example, is in places polished like a mirror.) Two stone griffins from the site, recognized as parts of a throne of Persian type, show the same polish. In 1912 a rough-and-ready attempt to uncover a large building produced Persian features of a more ample kind: a hall with upwards of eighty pillars which, though very fragmentary, were observed to have the same lustrous polish. Unsatisfactory though the evidence is in detail, it is sufficiently clear that we have here a Persian *diwan* or *apadana* or audience-hall, and that we are confronted once more with a deliberate 'Persianization' that bespeaks the

Ill. 131

presence of imported ideas and, no doubt, of imported master-masons.

Indeed the Pāṭaliputra palace may well have employed some part of the first generation of immigrant Persian craftsmen after the fall of the Achaemenid Empire. Today, however, the earliest upstanding vestiges of the Indo-Persian phase are the work of a second or third generation, and doubtless for the most part of Indian pupils and successors. These vestiges are the familiar commemorative pillars – originally more than thirty of them – which the great Ashoka, grandson of Chandragupta, set up in the middle of the third century BC after his conversion to Buddhism. Later, many of them were inscribed with Ashoka's pious precepts; but in origin they were uninscribed and were a continuation, in a new form, of an old-standing Indian custom, that of setting up posts, normally of timber, to commemorate a great victory or some special sacrifice, or to honour a deity such as Garuda-dhvaja. Behind all this seems to lie the Indian cosmic idea of a World Axis, conceived as a pillar separating heaven and earth. Where Ashoka's pillars differed from the normal run was in three respects: they were uniformly of stone, their symbolism was Buddhist or at least adopted by Buddhism, and they were derived from the Persian, so-called 'Persepolitan', type, with the typically Persian polish. In other words, the Buddhist king was using an alien, or recently naturalized, idiom to express an Indian idea.

Ill. 132

That he carried through this combined operation with success is amply indicated by the surviving pillars; above all, the greatest of the series, the lion-column of Sarnath which has been aptly taken as the badge of the Indian Republic. The lion was an epithet often applied to the Buddha, though it had earlier been a regal emblem which had found an honoured place in the architectural sculpture of Persia; and the wheel formerly carried by the

132, 133   The so-called bell-shaped or 'inverted lotus' capital seen in Indian architecture is the result of Persian influence. Perhaps the most famous example is the lion-column of Sarnath, left, erected by Ashoka about 250 BC and since taken as the badge of the Indian Republic. A more distinctively Indian form of the Ashokan bell-shaped capital of some two centuries later may be seen in the rock-cut Buddhist chaitya at Karli, right

lions was a symbol of imperial rule before it was adopted by the Buddha as the Wheel of the Buddhist Law.

Setting aside, however, the religious symbolism of the Ashokan pillars, we may emphasize their wider architectural significance. It is this: the so-called bell-shaped or 'inverted lotus' capital of these pillars is, on the one hand, Persian in origin and, on the other hand, entered widely into the construction of the Indian architectural 'orders' from the time of the Mauryans far into the Middle Ages – until, in fact, it yielded to the dominance of the Chālukyan lathe or the baroque fantasies of Vijayanagar. The elaborately fluted and enriched column-capitals, for

Ill. 133

134 This column-capital is basically of Persian type, but shows completely Indian motifs on both faces. Its date probably lies sometime in the third to second century BC. From Sarnath

example, hewn out of square piers in the sixth century AD by the rock-cutters of Badāmi, south of Bombay, retain the elements of this form more than eight centuries after its introduction into India; and even the plain or faceted capitals of Pallava and Choḷa architecture in the far south are derived ultimately from the same remote source.

Nor does the architectural link with Iran end there. In India, as in Iran, the weight of the architrave beam is commonly transmitted to the column through an oblong impost-block or bracket, spread laterally to take the strain, rather than through the square impost of the more classical orders of the West. These brackets varied in shape from age to age, and can to a considerable extent be classified chronologically. Some of them are elaborately carved into double or addorsed animal-forms which go back to the 'protomes' or double animals of the familiar Achaemenian imposts. Others are moulded into a variety

Ill. 134

Ill. 133

135 The entrance to the Lomas Rishi cave in the Barābar hills near Gayā in Bihār. These 'cave-buildings' were carved in the reign of Ashoka about 250 BC and are the earliest dated examples in India

of shapes which have close identical counterparts in ancient and modern Iran, shapes sufficiently numerous and specialized to suggest a historical link between the Persian and Indian traditions.

Finally, any consideration both of the indebtedness of India to Achaemenid Persia and of the extent to which India transmuted her borrowings must take account of rock-cut architecture and inscriptions. From the seventh century BC onwards, if not earlier, tombs in the likeness of pillared halls were being cut into the cliffs of Media and Persia. The rock-cut pillared shrines of India are famous, but the earliest dated 'cave-buildings' of India are those carved in the reign of Ashoka about 250 BC in the Barābar hills near Gayā in Bihār. The first attempts simulate vernacular types, though with the Persian polish; the sequence Persia-India is clear enough. Again, the Bisutūn or Behistūn rock-inscription of Darius I dates from about 518 BC; there is in India no precedent for the

Ill. 135

rock-edicts cut at the bidding of Ashoka in and after 257 BC. In these things the Mauryan emperor was deliberately adopting the methods of the Great Kings, whose mantle had in a sense descended upon him. But the resemblance is one of technique, not of aesthetic or spiritual content. Save for an occasional formula, nothing could be more unlike the commemorative and administrative records of the proud Persian despots than the gentle exhortations of the equally despotic but more humble-minded Buddhist king.

In such fashion civilization drew upon civilization, and the changing thought of India was both enriched by borrowed forms and formulae and disciplined by the element of continuity that borrowing implied. It is probable that no similar period in history has exercised a more profound influence upon the culture of the subcontinent than did the century which followed the fall of the Persian empire and the transit of Alexander the Great. In northern India many of the material elements of civilization were already present in the Gangetic towns before those events occurred; but it was only in the sequel, when the strong intelligence of Chandragupta and Ashoka, governed in the latter by an intensely Indian spirituality, gathered together the new threads and wove them into something like a national pattern, that a large part of India once more, after 2000 years, produced an integrated civilization.

136 An important administrative document, of the third century BC, this inscribed limestone slab from Mahāstān, East Bengal, records the measures taken by the local authority to combat a famine by the issue of paddy (rice) from reserve stocks

CHAPTER SIX

Eastern, Central and Southern India

East of Pāṭaliputra the moderate rainfall of the plains is doubled and shortly quintupled in intensity, and close marshy jungle barred the easy advance of civilization. Here, in Bengal, is evidence of the persistence of small disarticulate societies in an essentially neolithic condition long after the early metal-using towns of the Jumna-Ganges *doāb* had reached a measure of maturity. It was not indeed until the powerfully organized Mauryan regime thrust eastwards in the third century BC that, as the evidence goes, occasional towns of a substantial character began to emerge within the river-system of the Brahmaputra. They would appear however to have remained few in number until well into the Middle Ages. The most impressive of them is represented by the mounds and ruins of Puṇḍranagar, now Mahāsthān, in the Bogra district of East Bengal. Puṇḍranagar was the capital of the Puṇḍras, an ancient people who, like the Dasyūs of the Punjab, were regarded with contempt by the Aryan invaders. The site of their town has been inadequately explored in depth. Most of its known features belong to the time of the Guptas (fourth to seventh century AD) and later; but an important stone inscription is ascribed to the Mauryan period (third century BC) and indicates that the place was then an administrative centre. It refers to

Ill. 136

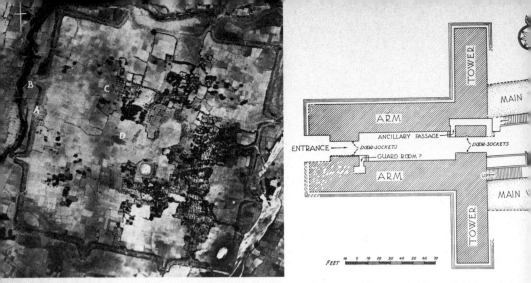

137-139 The plan of Shishupālgarh is extremely regular as may be seen in the aerial view, left. The wall was broken at intervals by eight principal gates (*Ills. 138, 139*), which show by their design that a military mind had considered the problem and also that ample resources for the building were at hand. It dates probably from Ashoka, about 260 BC

the common danger of floods in Bengal and the measures taken by the governor of Puṇḍranagar to meet it by the issue of paddy (rice) from reserve stocks evidently kept for the purpose. These stocks were to be replenished in better times both in kind and in coin – an interesting early reference to coinage, presumably of the punch-marked type found frequently in Bengal as in other parts of India. As a side-light on the economy of a period marked by administrative commonsense, the document is of notable historical interest.

For more material evidence of Mauryan urban expansion into eastern India, we have at present to go to Orissa where, on the outskirts of the temple-city of Bhubaneshwar, a fortified site known as Shishupālgarh has been shown by excavation to date in origin from the third

Ill. 137

century BC. Its plan is an extremely regular square, with sides each three-quarters of a mile long and defences consisting basically of an earthen rampart 30 ft high. Symmetrically in each side are two dramatically salient gateways of stone, and there seem to have been supplementary posterns. The regular spacing of the eight

principal portals may be assumed to indicate a grid-plan for the streets, though these have not yet been investigated. The portals, each intricately planned with two successive gates, a pedestrians' bypass and flanking walls or fighting-platforms, are built superbly of laterite blocks, and have every appearance (subject to verification) of belonging to an early period of the defences.

Ills. 138, 139

A regimented plan of this kind is exceptional in Indian architecture, and suggests both a military mind and ample resources. The most likely moment within the third century BC is immediately after Ashoka's famous victory over the Kalingas of this region, about 264 BC, when the foundation or re-foundation of such a city as a civilizing instrument of pacification would be entirely in character. The misery occasioned by the campaign, it will be recalled, turned the king into a determined pacifist and led to his conversion to Buddhism; it is historically improbable therefore that this fortress-town was built during the peaceful half-century following 264, whilst an earlier date is equally out of the question. Further excavation could not fail to be rewarding. Nor does Shishupālgarh stand alone in this matter. Seemingly at the same time, at Jaugaḍā in Ganjām district, southern Orissa, an Iron Age culture and an earthern rampart 25 ft high were imposed upon a site previously occupied by villagers equipped with stone axes. Jaugaḍā is less familiar than Shishupāl-garh but appears to share the same problems; and here again excavation may some day discover more evidence as to the great Ashoka's thinking at the turning point of his career.

Meanwhile in central India urban development had been less reluctant than in the north-east, though it would appear to have started later than in the Gangetic plain. Something has been said above about the busy village-communities which, along the Narbadā, in Malwa and elsewhere in the middle region between *c*. 2000 and 600 BC, exercised a chalcolithic technology, mostly based upon microliths supplemented by a little precious copper. It is increasingly apparent as we have seen, that beneath the markedly local and often lively elements of these cultures can be detected a measure of affinity, a cousin-ship, with chalcolithic cultures in the north-west. Like the chert or chalcedony blades and the copper flat axes (p. 89), the pottery is consistent with a slowly moving, intermittent connection down the west coast, always with local variation and experiment. And then, shortly before or after 500 BC, the developed urbanity of the Jumna-Ganges *doāb* descended upon the scene.

A crucial site is that of Ujjain, where recent digging has taken place. Ujjain, one of the sacred cities of India and capital of the ancient kingdom of Avanti (now Mālwā), lies beside the river Sipra, a tributary of the Chambal which is itself a tributary of the Jumna. It domi-nated the trunk-route from the *doāb* to the Arabian Sea and, as a developed city, was an early offshoot of the Ganges Civilization. It is of a roughly pentagonal plan, with major axes of about a mile. Its massive mud ram-

140 At Ujjain, one of the sacred cities of India, the massive defences at one point ran alongside the river. In order to break the force of the flow of the current as it struck the 40-foot-high rampart, reinforcing timber breakwaters were set diagonally to the stream. The banks were repaired at various intervals with mud and baked brick

part is 250 ft wide at the base and upwards of 40 ft high; this, beside the river where it catches the full flow of the current, was reinforced by timber breakwaters set diagonally to the stream, and there are later repairs both of mud and of baked brick. Outside the rampart, except where the river rendered additional work unnecessary, there is a formidable fosse, originally 150 ft wide at the top and 20 ft deep. From the material of the rampart were recovered the two southernmost sherds of Painted Grey Ware, and iron occurred in the lowest of the related strata. Within the line of the defences were buildings of stone and baked brick with ring-wells or soak-pits which have already been noted as characteristic of Indian towns from the latter half of the first millennium BC onwards. In one of the gates, the roadway had been metalled and re-metalled on numerous occasions, and bore the ruts of carts with the universal gauge of about 5 ft 9 ins.

On present knowledge, Ujjain suggests a relatively sudden projection of the civilization of the northern plains upon a site previously occupied, if at all, by a purely local settlement of small-town or village status. Farther south, on the other hand, at Maheshwar, the evidence is clear enough. Here, where the Ujjain trunk-route crossed the Narbadā, there was, as noted above, a

Ill. 140

considerable and lengthy chalcolithic occupation on both banks of the river before the fully evolved technology of the Ganges Civilization was suddenly imposed upon the more northerly site, that of Maheshwar itself. There was no transition between the lower and the higher culture; the latter swept down and smothered the former with a twenty-foot accumulation of buildings, soak-pits, iron implements, Northern Black Polished Ware, and organized equipment which included a sprinkling of punch-marked coins as witness to an organized commerce wholly alien to the preceding Chalcolithic. The point need not be laboured: civilization arrived in central India with a bang: it came from the Jumna-Ganges *doāb* along the natural traffic-lines through the Vindhya Range, and it reached the Narbadā – the east-west axis of central India – by the beginning of the fifth century BC.

The extension of civilization southwards into the heart of the Deccan and peninsular India runs parallel with that already noticed in Bengal and Orissa. There is no reason for ascribing it to a period earlier than the third century BC, and, at something more than a guess, it can be associated with the southward extension of the Mauryan Empire by Bindusāra, father of Ashoka, at the beginning of that century. On two town-sites, namely Maski in Raichur district, in Andhra Pradesh, and Brahmagiri, the ancient Isila, farther south in Mysore State, the main characters of this peninsular civilization have been observed with care. At both sites there are Ashokan rock-cut edicts; at both, the advent of civilization is the advent also of iron; at both, a Black-and-Red Ware which, as we have seen, has roots in the chalcolithic of Saurashtra and Rājasthān now joins the main southward spread, which in some regions it had in fact anticipated; at both, the rites of the dead included the erection of megalithic cists or monuments, the origin of which is in dispute and need not be discussed here; at both there is a sharp cultural

Ill. 141

141 The majority of Indian megalith tombs are found in the south of the country. The example illustrated, from Brahma-giri, Mysore, is of the type known as a 'port-hole' cist, taking its name from the round 'port-hole' opening which may be seen, blocked, at the head, the eastern end, of the cist. These cists, or chests, are built of granite (sometimes laterite) slabs within a stone circle and are about 6 feet in length

cleavage between the richly equipped Iron Age and the semi-barbarous chalcolithic or neolithic substratum which has been traced back as far as the third millennium. From now on the Peninsula was in the main stream of civilization, varied by those remarkable backwaters where, in the hills and forests, ancient tribal societies have remained to modern times as a familiar archaism in the Indian scene.

But this was not quite the end of the rise of civilization in India. Mention must be added of one further tributary to the main stream; the vigorous Graeco-Roman trade which, from the first century BC–AD, brought a wealth of sophisticated European goods and contacts into central and peninsular India, in exchange for local Indian cloths, semi-precious stones, pearls and, above all, spices, and occasionally even Chinese silks. This trade, known to us from Greek, Roman and Indian literature and, less amply but quite definitely, from material evidence, struck both coasts of the Peninsula at a number of recorded places. Amongst them, at Muziris (probably Cranganore on the Cochin inlets) the fourth century map known as the Peutinger Table marks a 'temple of Augustus'. This has not yet been found, but on the opposite side of India, on the Coromandel coast, the Indo-French town of Pondi-cherry (anciently Pudu-chcheri or Newtown) has been

Ills. 142–144

142 A bronze statuette of Hercules-Serapis, from Begram, Afghanistan, shows him standing, resting his right hand on a knotted club and wearing a modius or corn-measure on his head. This emblem is normally characteristic of Jupiter-Serapis, who was revered as god of the corn supply as well as a god of the dead

Ill. 143
Ill. 144

identified with the *Podoukē* of Ptolemy and the Greek *Periplus*, and excavators have identified the ancient site (under the folk-name of Arikamedu) nearby. It is of interest to observe that here the replacement of a purely native village by a substantial brick-built town coincided with the arrival of Western trade-goods in quantity, including amphorae of wine and the bright red table-wares of Arretium in Tuscany. Incidentally, some of the amphorae, when found, were still coated internally with a resin deposit derived, no doubt, from their former contents, the *retsina* or resinated wine which still attracts or repels the visitor to the Greek end of the Mediterranean. In one way and another, the impact of this commerce from the centres of European civilization may be supposed to have played a part in the development of skills and the widening of horizons that stimulated the somewhat tardy upgrowth of urban life in the southern part of the subcontinent.

CHAPTER SEVEN

Summary

Finally, let us summarize this progressive pervasion of civilized life through two and a half thousand years and the two million square miles of a great subcontinent. The story began in the middle of the third millennium, when social ideas which had been elaborated in Mesopotamia fertilized certain of the lively but limited chalcolithic communities of the Baluch-Indus borderland and produced the seemingly sudden flowering of Phase I of Indian civilization, that specifically of the Indus valley. By the end of the millennium the Indus Civilization was dominating the western coastlands from Makran in the north to the Gulf of Cambay and the Narbadā-Kim estuaries far to the south, either by spontaneous expansion or under pressures (commercial or other) which cannot be closely defined. Certainly well before the middle of the second millennium (about 1700 BC) internal decay, stimulated perhaps by geomorphological changes and periodical flooding, had set in, and had prepared the way – at least at Mohenjo-daro – for a violent end by raiders of one sort or another. Whether these raiders were the nomadic Aryans whose inroads into the Punjab are reflected in the Vedic hymns is a matter for conjecture, but a certain parallelism between their recorded exploits and the archaeological evidence can be adduced.

At Chanhu-daro and Amrī, in Sind, the Civilization was succeeded by low-grade cultures with some affinities in north-western Asia. Meanwhile to the south and east, along the coast of Kāthiāwāḍ or Saurashtra, a significantly different sequel has been observed.

Here the mature Indus or Harappā civilization was variously transmuted into a new chalcolithic small-town phase which shows links with second millennium village-life in central India. Sometime during that millennium evidence emerged of a developed and individual copper industry centred upon the Gangetic lands but at present of undefined context. Equally nebulous in origin but of wider significance is the developing urban life which appears within the same region during the earlier half of the first millennium B C. There, in the homeland of the Indian epics, flowered Phase II of Indian civilization, to which the name Ganges Civilization may reasonably be applied. The Phase marks the beginning of the use of iron and the beginning of continuous civilization in the northern plains. Until somewhere about 500 B C its characteristic industry was the production of the very distinctive Painted Grey Ware.

This important urban development was supplemented and stimulated in the latter half of the sixth century B C by fresh influences of a civilizing kind which entered the north-western corner of the subcontinent in the train of the Achaemenid kings of Persia. Their colonization of the frontier region brought security to the trade-routes thereabouts, prosperity to the towns along them – Begram near Kabul, Chārsada near Peshāwar, Taxila near Rawalpindi – and an improved equipment which included coinage. These benefits were not slow in reaching out to the now-flourishing cities of the *doāb*. Here substantial buildings of baked brick began to replace the mud-brick structures normal to the earlier phase; and incidentally, perhaps in literal imitation of the polished

143, 144 Arretine ware, left, the bright red table-ware from Arretium in Tuscany, travelled far beyond the Roman Imperial frontiers in trade with the East. These sherds are from Arikamedu, near Pondicherry. The base, left centre, has a potter's mark. Fragments of amphorae from the Mediterranean, the tali pottery vessels with pointed bases for carrying wine, were also found at the same site, right. First centuries BC–AD

surface of an abundant iron industry, the celebrated Northern Black Polished Ware, with its steel-like gloss, came into vogue as a prophetic aid to the archaeologists of the future. The new modes and techniques, however, implied at first no radical revolution in the life of the great plains; rather they confirmed and amplified the civilizing trends already at work there. The period after 500 BC and more particularly after 300 BC was one of enrichment, economically and culturally; a trend which culminated in the rise of the Mauryan Empire as a 'successor state' to the Persian Empire after the transit of Alexander the Great. The Mauryans inherited and at the same time transmuted Achaemenid political and cultural ideas and made good use of unemployed Persian talent. A notable example of this process was the importation of Persian architectural forms which were to influence the religious architecture of India far into the Middle Ages.

Phase III might better be described as a sub-phase of Phase II. It represents the southward thrust of the maturing Ganges Civilization towards central India; in particular, to the Narbadā valley, through which an outlet was thus secured to the harbours of the west coast. This thrust occurred not later than the fifth century B C, and may be regarded perhaps as a material aspect of that flowering of the intellect and the spirit which found expression in the outgrowth of Buddhism and Jainism from the same Gangetic homeland.

Phase IV has a more substantive quality. It was, if the evidence is read aright, essentially a product of the southerly extension of the Mauryan Empire from the Ganges at the beginning of the third century B C. Over a congeries of chalcolithic cultures with a strongly microlithic bias swept the fully developed Gangetic Iron Age, represented by emissaries on a sufficiently small scale to absorb local traditions whilst imposing the (literally) iron discipline of the northern civilization. For the moment this advance petered out in northern Mysore, but it later reached the southern end of the Peninsula and by the first century A D, was fully established there, with widespread and stimulating contacts overseas. Starting at about the same time, that is, the third century B C, it began to spread also down the coastal plains beside the eastern ghats (Ashoka's famous conquest of the Kalingas of Orissa about 264 B C is a key-point), and as far south as the famous Amarāvatī on the Krishna river the Northern Black Polished Ware of the Ganges found an ultimate home. The picture of gradual pervasion from north to south is a logical and integral one. Thenceforth, Indian civilization becomes a proper and primary study for the historian, with the archaeologist now in a subordinate though still useful role.

Bibliography

General Works

BASHAM, A.L. *The Wonder that was India*, London, 1954
CHILDE, V.G. *New Light on the Most Ancient East*, 4th ed., London, 1952
GORDON, D.H. *The Prehistoric Background of Indian Culture*, Bombay, 1958
KOSAMBI, D.D. *The Culture and Civilization of Ancient India*, London, 1965
PIGGOTT, S. *Prehistoric India*, London, 1950
WHEELER, SIR MORTIMER *Early India and Pakistan*, London, 1959
— *The Indus Civilization*, 2nd ed., Cambridge, 1960

More Specialized Works

BOSE, N.K., and others. *Human Skeletal Remains from Harappā*, Anthropological Survey of India, Calcutta, 1963
CASAL, J.-M. *Fouilles d'Amri*, Paris, 1964 (with English summary)
DALES, G.F. Harappan Outposts on the Makran Coast, *Antiquity* XXXVI (1962), 86–92
KRAMER, S.N. Dilmun: Quest for Paradise, *Antiquity* XXXVII (1963), 111–115
MACKAY, E.J.H. *Further Excavations at Mohenjo-daro*, Delhi, 1938
— *Chanhu-daro Excavations* 1935–36, American Oriental Soc., New Haven, Connecticut, 1943
MALLOWAN, M.E.L. The Mechanics of Ancient Trade in Western Asia, *Iran III* (1965), 1–7
MARSHALL, J. *Mohenjo-daro and the Indus Civilization*, London, 1931
— *Taxila*, Cambridge, 1951
OPPENHEIM, A.L. The Sea-faring Merchants of Ur, *Journ. of American Oriental Soc.*, 74 (1954), 6–17
RAIKES, R.L. The End of the Ancient Cities of the Indus, *American Anthropologist*, vol. 66, no. 2, April 1964
SANKALIA, H.D. *Prehistory and Protohistory in India and Pakistan*, University of Bombay, 1962. With special reference to central India
VATS, M.S. *Excavations at Harappā*, Delhi, 1940
WHEELER, SIR MORTIMER Harappā 1946: the Defences and Cemetery R 37, *Ancient India*, no. 3 (Delhi, 1947), 58–130
— Iran and India in pre-Islamic Times, *Ancient India*, no. 4, Delhi, 1948, 85–103
— *Rome beyond the Imperial Frontiers*, London, 1954

List of Illustrations

The author and publishers are grateful to the many official bodies, institutions and individuals mentioned below for their assistance in supplying original illustration material. Photographs without acknowledgement are by courtesy of the author.

139

63 Grotesque terracotta figurine of a woman from Mohenjo-daro. Approximately actual size

64 Terracotta 'flook-like' figure holding its muzzle from Mohenjo-daro. Approximately actual size. National Museum of Pakistan, Karachi

65 Chert blades and cores from Mohenjo-daro. Approximately actual size

66 Copper fish-hooks from Mohenjo-daro

67 Copper arrowhead from Mohenjo-daro. Drawn by Phillip Ward

68 Copper flat-axes from Mohenjo-daro

69 Copper shaft-hole adze-axe from Mohenjo-daro. National Museum of Pakistan, Karachi

70 Indus Valley beads of gold, faience, carnelian and steatite. National Museum of Pakistan, Karachi. Photo Josephine Powell

71 Necklaces and bracelet from Mohenjo-daro; gold and semi-precious stones

72 Indus Valley beads: 1–4, 6, 7, steatite, 5, carnelian, 8, gold, 9–11 and 16, faience, 13, agate, 12, 14, terracotta, 15, shell. After Wheeler

73 Bronze pins and carnelian beads, from Mohenjo-daro. National Museum of Pakistan, Karachi. Photo Josephine Powell

74 Black-on-red painted vase from cemetery R37, Harappā. National Museum of Pakistan, Karachi

75 Pottery vase and plate from cemetery H, Harappā

76 Goblet with potter's mark from Harappā

77 Painted pottery from Mohenjo-daro. National Museum of Pakistan, Karachi. Photo Josephine Powell

78 Pre-Indus culture sherds from beneath the citadel at Harappā

79 'Nal' style pottery from Baluchistan. British Museum. Photo Eileen Tweedy

80 Fishing on the Indus. Photo courtesy of Dr George F. Dales

81 'Persian Gulf' seal and impression from Lothal. National Museum, New Delhi. Photo courtesy Archaeological Survey of India

82 Boring at Mohenjo-daro, 1964–5. Photo courtesy of Dr George F. Dales

83 Excavations in the lower levels, Mohenjo-daro, 1950

84 Flooded excavations in the lower levels, Mohenjo-daro, 1950

85 Late walls (on earthen supports) built when the ground-level had risen to the top of the granary, Mohenjo-daro

86 Buildings of later phases built above the original level of the granary, Mohenjo-daro

87 Late-period well standing high above lower-level buildings, Mohenjo-daro. Photo courtesy of Dr R. Hodson

88, Skeletons of massacre victims in the
89 upper levels of Room 74, House V, 'HR Area' of Mohenjo-daro

90 Two skeletons of massacre victims in a street in 'DK Area', Mohenjo-daro

91 Skeletons of massacre victims in a lane in 'HR Area', Mohenjo-daro. Found by Dr George F. Dales, 1964

Index

Numbers in italics refer to illustrations

143